Stopping the Storm of Anger

Before it Stops You

Larry Huch

STOPPING THE STORM OF ANGER
BEFORE IT STOPS YOU
By Larry Huch

ISBN 10: 0-9792565-9-3
ISBN 13: 978-0-9792565-9-2
Copyright © 2008

Larry Huch Ministries
P.O. Box 610890
Dallas, TX 75261
www.larryhuchministries.com

Dedication

This book is dedicated to my family.
To my children and their spouses:
Anna & Brandin, Luke & Jen, and Katie;
to my twin grand-sugars, Asher & Judah; and as
always, to my wife Tiz, my BER SHEAT.

I can't tell you often enough how very proud I am of all
of you. Your constant example of faith, love, and
dedication to the Lord and to His people brings
honor, joy, and purpose to my life.

I love you all.

TABLE OF CONTENTS

INTRODUCTION 7

1 THE BAIT 11

2 DON'T TAKE IT! 25

3 INSECURITY: A RESULT OF OFFENSE 37

4 RAGE: THE SILENT EPIDEMIC 53

5 BITTERNESS: THE ROOT OF ANGER 63

6 THE ROOTS OF BITTERNESS: JEALOUSY AND ENVY 69

7 THE ROOTS OF BITTERNESS: NOT FORGIVING OTHERS 75

8 THE ROOTS OF BITTERNESS: NOT FORGIVING YOURSELF . . 81

9 THE HIGH PRICE OF ANGER 85

10 STOPPING THE STORM OF ANGER 95

INTRODUCTION

It is so important in these last days, that we thoroughly understand our positioning in the Kingdom and in the history of time. We are entering into Jubilee...the beginning of the Sabbath Millennium. It is critically important that we move beyond focusing on what we were saved *from* and begin focusing on what we were saved *for*.

It is the will of God that we win. We are created to be winners. We are more than overcomers, yet many of the people of God are not walking in His blessing. Why?

If we are to truly move forward and get on with the business of living and soul-winning and fulfilling our divine destiny, we must acknowledge and overcome anything that may be holding us back. Two of the major things holding back the children of God today is taking offense and becoming angry. It is not possible that we can go through life with no one offending us. We might as well face it, people will offend us, but we do have the option of not taking that offense and becoming angry people.

If we choose to take offense, it negatively affects our character. A negative character is not Christ-like and God cannot move us into a position of high visibility if our character is an embarrassment to Jesus Christ. We must have a Godly character, free of offense, if we are to fulfill what we have been designed to do.

Offended people are angry people, and an angry person is not a blessed person. Anger will stop the blessings of God in our life.

It is not easy to be a person who is free of offense. In Romans 7:15, the Apostle Paul says, *"For what I am doing, I do not understand. For what I will to do, that I do not practice; but what I hate, that I do."* He's saying, "Why am I like this? Why can't I consistently do what I know is right?" Sound familiar?

Paul goes on to say, *"If, then, I do what I will not to do, I agree with the law that it is good. But now, it is no longer I who do it, but sin* [bondage] *that dwells in me. For I know that in me (that is, in my flesh) nothing good dwells; for to will is present with me, but how to perform what is good I do not find. For the good that I will to do, I do not do; but the evil I will not to do, that I practice. Now if I do what I will not to do, it is no longer I who do it, but sin that dwells in me. I find then a law, that evil is present with me, the one who wills to do good. For I delight in the law of God according to the inward man. But I see another law in my members, warring against the law of my mind, and bringing me into captivity to the law of sin which is in my members. O wretched man that I am! Who will deliver me from this body of death?"*

And then the answer comes: *"I thank God—through Jesus Christ our Lord!"* Jesus Christ our Lord! That means "through The Anointed One with the burden-lifting, yoke destroying power of Almighty God." Through our Lord. That is the answer.

I know many of you who are reading this book have felt exactly like this. "I know what's right. I want to do what is right, but I can't do it! I know the difference between right and wrong, but I do the wrong instead of what I know is right. I am in bondage. How can I be set free?"

Before we can truly be free from something, we have to acknowledge its existence and influence in our life, then we need to confess it. James 5:16 tells us to confess our faults one to another. Now a fault is an imperfection or a flaw that lies below the surface. It is one of those hidden things, the things very few people ever see. It lies beneath the Sunday morning look of suits, ties, pretty dresses and nice makeup. It lies under the 40-pound Bible we carry and the 30-pound cross around our neck. Those hidden things are what James is talking about, and he says we must confess it. Confess that hidden thing!

It is very difficult to confess our faults because we have been taught that we are to be perfect. From the moment we get saved, we should be just like Jesus. Let me tell you something: The moment you are like Jesus, you won't be here any more. Since you are still here, you can safely assume you are not like Him! It is not a miracle; it is a miracle process.

No one decides on purpose, when they are a child, that they want to be a bad person. We need to realize our enemy. Once we see that having a fault does not make us a bad person, we can have great liberty to confess those faults. I am not a bad person, you are not a bad person. We do things we do not want to do because of something that landed on us. The sin nature has been passed on since the time of Adam through no choice of our own.

From this place of wanting to do what is right, but being in bondage, it is impossible to just say no. It cannot be done. It requires a miracle from the burden-removing, yoke-destroying power of God. He not only removes the burden of our sins from us, but He goes on to destroy the yoke of bondage that causes us to continue to do what we don't want to do.

Now don't forget that Paul was a Christian and a leader in the church when he wrote about this great dilemma. He was not writing to a bunch of non-christians, he was writing to the church. He was not belaboring his past or bemoaning his present. God inspired him to write this for our future.

One of the times Tiz and I were on TBN, our good friends, LaVerne and Edith Tripp were hosting the show. I had told LaVerne that so many people had heard my testimony about being delivered from selling drugs, taking drugs, and the crimes associated with that lifestyle, that I really didn't want to make it the focus of this program.

During the show, LaVerne said, "I know you said you didn't want to talk about your testimony, but I feel there is something the Lord wants you to share." Suddenly I found myself talking about the problem I, as a Christian and a Pastor, have had with the spirit of anger. Now, people are ok with someone being delivered from a life of drugs or crime; but when you tell people you were a wife abuser or a child abuser, or a violent person, they're not nearly as excited.

This teaching is a direct result of that God-inspired program. It is my prayer that you, too, will be set free to move on toward the fulfillment of your divine destiny.

—Pastor Larry Huch

Chapter 1
The Bait

Before we can deal with the spirit of anger, we need to look at the problem of taking offense; simply because anger will stem from offenses. If anger is a trap — and it is — then offense is the bait. In Matthew 24, the Bible gives us a scene where Jesus is walking with His disciples: *"Now as He sat on the Mount of Olives, the disciples came to Him privately, saying, 'Tell us, when will these things be? And what will be the sign of Your coming, and of the end of the age?'"*

First, let me say that we are heading into the Sabbath millennium. The Jews are gathering in the land of Israel, waiting for the messiah to come. Everything is lining up. More than 2,000 years ago, the disciples said to Jesus, "Lord, what's the sign of Your coming?" Now, we all know about wars and rumors of wars, but look at the end of this story. I've seen it before, but it never grabbed me until I started an in-depth study on this subject.

After talking about the earthquakes, famines, diseases, and wars that He calls "the beginning of sorrows," Jesus answers them, *"And then many will be offended, will betray one another, and will hate one another."* The very last thing

Jesus told the disciples would be a sign of His coming was that offenses will multiply. If you study that scripture in depth, it means that in the last days a spirit of offense will be released — and He is not only talking about the world.

Whether you're in the ministry or working a nine-to-five job, being angry and offended can and will stop your destiny. Being offended is a choice. The bait is offered, but that doesn't mean you have to walk into the trap!

In the book of Luke we see that Jesus again is talking with His disciples. Let me point out that this is Jesus Christ speaking — the most powerful, positive-confessing faith teacher there ever was. He said, "It's impossible that you won't be offended." (Luke 17:1) Jesus said it 2,000 years ago. "It is impossible." Whether you're old or young; black or white; tall or short; long-haired or bald; whether you're in church or at work; walking the streets or driving in a car; it is impossible that you won't be offended. So the question today is not, "Will I be offended?" Yes, you will be offended. It's going to happen. It may happen before you get to your car. It may happen through a sinner on the street. It may happen through somebody in the church. Somehow you will be given the opportunity to be offended.

I was preaching in Phoenix, and a man got offended and walked out because somebody sat in his chair. A friend of mine said, "This brother gets up every morning wondering who's going to offend him, and I'm sure he's never disappointed!" When you look for offense; you'll never be disappointed. Some offenses are imaginary. Some are accidental. Somebody may say or do something to you that may unintentionally offend you, but there was no harm or malice in their heart.

Let me give you an example: I'm right handed, so I always carry my Bible or briefcase in my right hand. Once while I was preaching in another country, somebody reached out to shake my hand. Now all my things were in my right hand, so instead of taking the time to shift everything over, I simply gave them my left hand. To make a long story short, that person was highly offended. I had no idea why until somebody later told me that reaching out your left hand in greeting is a major insult in that country.

Sometimes a major offense is totally accidental. We can't ignore, though, that sometimes they're done on purpose. The devil is going to use people to offend you. They're going to call you names or do things intentionally to hurt you. The question is, "Will you allow yourself to be offended?" The devil's attempts to offend you are not optional. Your acceptance of the offenses, on the other hand, is optional. It is a matter of choice. When offenses come and start to multiply, will you choose to take them and miss the promises of God?

The Bible says the devil is like a roaring lion, roaming around looking for someone whom he may devour. (1 Peter 5:8) The Bible gives us a response: *"This is the day that the Lord has made. Let us rejoice and be glad in it."* (Psalm 118:24) and *"The joy of the Lord is your strength."* (Nehemiah 8:10) If the devil steals your joy, then he has stolen your strength to make it into the Promised Land, or the land where God wants to fulfill all He has promised to you. The joy of the Lord is what keeps you strong. So the devil is going to find somebody he can use to steal your joy, but the Bible says, "Rejoice"! If the horse bucks you off; RE-mount! If your gun is empty; RE-load! If you've lost your joy; RE-joice!

Philippians 4:4 says, *"Rejoice in the Lord always."* So when the devil comes in, he may borrow our joy, but he doesn't get to keep it! This is why the Bible says, *"Be angry and sin not."* (Ephesians 4:26) If somebody offends you by speaking falsely against you, it's going to try and steal your joy. You will feel the hurt inside of you. When they hung Jesus on the cross, they said, *"Crucify him!"* These were the same people He healed. You know He felt that hurt inside, but He responded with love instead of lashing out in anger. Let me say it again: He responded in love. He said, *"Father, forgive them, for they know not what they do."* (Luke 23:34) He chose to respond to them instead of reacting.

And so the Bible says, *"Rejoice in the Lord always."* Now if we never had to rejoice, He wouldn't have said, "always." When you are offended or something bad happens, rejoice, rejoice, rejoice, rejoice! Why? Because the joy of the Lord is your strength, and you can't afford to let the devil steal your strength.

In Philippians 4:8, Paul tells us how to restore our joy: *"Finally, brethren, whatever things are true, whatever things are noble, whatever things are just, whatever things are pure, whatever things are lovely, whatever things are of good report, if there is any virtue and if there is anything praiseworthy — meditate on these things."* And when you think on these things, *"the God of peace will be with you."* But if you don't, and you react to the hurt or offense, and you start stroking it and nurturing it and holding it and sharing it and multiplying it, then the God of peace isn't with you anymore. The one who has come to steal, kill, and destroy, begins to live in your conversation, your life, and your family. At that moment, we need to come to our senses. We have to RE-load and RE-mount by RE-joicing.

Now, we have learned that offenses will come. It's not because you're a bad person; it's because offenses will and do multiply. One of the primary evidences of offense is that we become angry. Anger will *always* cause us to miss out on the Promised Land.

Moses was one of the greatest men of the Bible and in the history of the world, but Numbers chapter 20 tells us what happened when this great man of God became offended. *"Then the children of Israel, the whole congregation, came into the Wilderness of Zin in the first month, and the people stayed in Kadesh; and Miriam died there and was buried there. Now there was no water for the congregation; so they gathered together against Moses and Aaron."*

Let's stop and look closely at something. In the Bible there were times when people lost their destiny by getting offended at God or at the men or women of God. In this passage we see Moses leading the Children of Israel out of Egypt. This is the same guy who gave up the palace, the same one who stood before Pharaoh, the same one who brought them out of 400 years bondage and the same guy who parted the Red Sea. Now they're in the desert. There's no water, and they're mad at Moses because there's no water — as if Moses is the water maker!

See, this is human nature. If we're going to be what God wants us to be and go where God wants us to go, then we absolutely have to be people who go beyond this kind of mentality.

Now look at this, "*And the people contended with* [argued with or blamed] *Moses and spoke, saying: 'If only we had died when our brethren died before the LORD! Why have you brought up the assembly of the LORD into this wilderness, that we and our animals should die here? And why have you made us come up out of Egypt, to bring us to this evil place? It is not a place of grain or figs or vines or pomegranates; nor is there any water to drink.'*"

Now let's stop right here. When you become angry or you become offended, it always makes you want to go back to the old places. The reason why they came out of Egypt is because there were no figs, there were no vines, and there was no fruit. There was no blessing! That's why they came out.

The reason why we came out of the bars and the world is because there was no peace, there was no joy, there was no happiness, and there was no blessing. That's why we came out. If we become offended in our marriage or with our children or with our mom or with our dad or with the church, the first thing the devil does is try to get us out of the land of abundant fruit and back into the leeks and the garlic and blame somebody while we're back there. Then we want somebody to come back with us to share in our pity party.

In the next verse it goes on to say, "*So Moses and Aaron went from the presence of the assembly to the door of the tabernacle of meeting, and they fell on their faces. And the glory of the LORD appeared to them.*

16

"Then the LORD spoke to Moses, saying, 'Take the rod; you and your brother Aaron gather the congregation together. Speak to the rock before their eyes, and it will yield its water; thus you shall bring water for them out of the rock, and give drink to the congregation and their animals.' So Moses took the rod from before the LORD as He commanded him.

"And Moses and Aaron gathered the assembly together before the rock; and he said to them, 'Hear now, you rebels!'" Now watch the progression of this. They're mad at Moses and Moses is mad at them. In reality, God was taking care of everything.

There's no reason to point fingers at Moses. We get mad at our husband. We get mad at our wife. We get mad at the guy at work. We get mad at the guy on the highway. When we get offended and get mad, we always miss the blessing.

It is so important that we get God's perspective on this. For example, let's say there's a person who smokes, but they're kind, loving, generous and full of compassion, Now here is this other guy who doesn't smoke or cuss but he gossips, is mean, is a racist, is prejudiced, angry, bitter, and resentful. Now which one is more Christ-like? It's the one who is kind and loving and gracious. You just can't be both Christ-like and mean. It just can't happen. Now remember, offense or anger is the bait in the trap that will snare you so you can't make it into the promised land, or the land where everything God has promised you is waiting. ***Don't take that bait.***

God wants His people to be lifted up. The problem is if God lifts us up, our positive and negative traits are amplified. The higher we go, the more we're seen. The more we're seen, the more our goodness is amplified. At the same time, the more our imperfections are amplified.

We'll never be perfect, but we can be mature. That's what the word *perfect* means. It means *mature*. It means we won't take offense. It means we won't be angry. It means we won't gossip. It means we won't slander. It means we won't kill somebody with our tongue. That's what that means.

Maybe God has your financial breakthrough set aside and waiting, but He can't give it to you because you gossip. It's right there in His word. In fact, God said you can bring all the tithes you want and still not be blessed because you're damaging your brother.

Verse 10 says, *"And Moses and Aaron gathered the assembly together before the rock; and he said to them, 'Hear now, you rebels!'"* Moses is upset! Pastor Moses is ticked off! *"Must we bring water for you out of this rock? Then Moses lifted his hand and struck the rock twice with his rod and water came out abundantly, and the congregation and their animals drank. Then the LORD spoke to Moses and Aaron, 'Because you did not believe Me,* [the word "believe" means to obey] *to hallow Me in the eyes of the children of Israel, therefore you shall not bring this assembly into the land which I have given them.'"* Let's look at that again. *"Because you did not...hallow Me in the eyes of the children."* Listen, if I'm laying hands on people and I'm seeing people healed, and delivered, but I'm a jerk while I'm driving and giving people certain hand signals that don't mean "one way," God said He is going to have to move me down the ladder!

God wants to lift His children up financially, politically and spiritually. But if you're going around telling people, "Jesus saves" and they hear us yelling at our wife or cussing at our husband, He can't lift us up. He has to keep us down. He wants us to go into the promised land, but we can't.

Let's think about Moses. He gave up the palace to be what God wanted him to be. He took care of the sheep in the desert for 40 years. Moses had the courage after he met with God in the burning bush, to stand before Pharaoh, the man who could have snuffed his life out, and say, *"Let my people go."* Moses took his rod and smote the waters and parted the Red Sea, but Moses never got to go into the promised land that God had prepared for him. The rest of the congregation went in. When you get offended; when you get angry at somebody, it doesn't stop their blessing; it only stops yours. I promise you, it will stop yours.

This was by no means Moses' first problem with the spirits of offense and anger. Much earlier in his life, he saw an Egyptian beating a Hebrew, so he killed him. God never told Moses to kill the guy, but Moses' anger rose up and struck the Egyptian dead. On another occasion, Moses was coming down the mountain from spending 40 days in the awesome presence of God. Upon seeing the golden calf the Hebrews had built as an idol, he got mad again at the people and threw the stones containing the Ten Commandments which God had just given him. Not only did he throw them, but he threw them down so hard they broke. You know that was some serious anger if he broke rocks!

Now he's standing there again, and God says, "Speak to the rock." Moses is mad and hits the rock. Now notice, this is where we get in trouble. The Bible says if you are angry with your brother, you're in danger of judgment. Well, it won't send you to hell, but your destiny will be altered. Your future will be altered. It will burn up instead of being released to us; to the church. Why? Because as Christians, we either bring shame to the name of God or bring glory to the name of God. There is no middle ground. It is one or the other. As we've already seen, God will not put us in a position of high-visibility if our character is not Christ-like.

Moses was not able to enter into the promises of God because of offenses. That's the very reason why most people aren't blessed today. Moses brought them out of slavery and the whole time they were coming out of Egypt, you don't see in the Word of God where they're saying, "Thanks Moses. You're the man!" No, they're just coming out. They're happy and singing praises, but the moment they get to the Red Sea, and the problem comes up, they say, "You brought us here to die! It's your fault!"

Then they get across the Red Sea and we don't read about one, "Thank you Moses for leading us." Forget about Moses! Do you understand what I'm saying? Then they go into the wilderness and there's no water. They say, "We're going to die!" Then God brings water out of the rock. Then there's no food and again they say, "We're going to die!" You don't see a whole lot of "Hey, good job, Moses." Every time something went wrong, they blamed Moses. And I'm sure Moses is sitting back in his tent thinking, "I'd like to give a whole new meaning to laying on of hands on these folks!"

We've got to be more mature than this. Are you understanding this? All because in all the years of his life, Moses never learned to control his anger, at the time when he was steps from the land of promise — the place of his greatest fulfillment — God said, "You're not going in, because you did not represent Me the right way."

This is what God is saying to us. This is a spiritual breakthrough. We're getting ready to go into the land of our greatest fulfillment. I'm not talking about heaven or the rapture. I'm talking about living in the blessings promised in Deuteronomy 28; about being the head and not the tail; being above and not beneath; being the lender and not the borrower!

In Acts 24:16, Paul says, "*I myself always strive to have a conscience without offense toward God and men.*" Notice he said he has to strive. He had to work at it. Now this is not some baby Christian who doesn't know how to walk with God — this is Paul, the apostle.

I have to exercise myself not to be offended and not to get angry. I have to work on this area in my life. Why? Because I love God so much? Yes, that's part of it. But it's also because I love me so much! There are great rewards for making sure that I don't get offended. You have to work at it. Tell yourself, "I will not be offended. I will not be offended." Offenses may come and offer us the trap, but we have to make sure we work on not taking the bait!

Do you know that Jesus had every right to be angry and offended? Do you know He had to work on it as much as we do? He was human which means He was born with a human nature. The very people that He healed, fed and delivered, were the ones crying out,

"Crucify him!" He was hanging there, and they were spitting on Him. He was God, yes, but He was just like you and I. As they spit on Him, He had to have been saying to Himself, "I battle not against flesh and blood, I battle not against flesh and blood!" He had to have been. He had to work on it.

And yet Jesus says, *"Follow Me." Follow Me* means *imitate Me* or *walk in the exact steps that I walk.* Do you know what He is saying? "They offended Me; they're going to offend you." The master is not servant to the slave; the created does not rule over the creator, and yet Jesus never took offense. Never. If Jesus can live without taking offense, so can we. First, because it's the Godly thing to do. Second, because the offense leads you into a trap that will rob you of your blessing.

You remember in the old cowboy movies, they're going along and the scout says, "Looks like a trap ahead." So they decide not to go in there. That's what we need to do: decide not to go in there.

The devil is there; he's like a roaring lion. He sets traps. So when somebody or something offends you, whether it is imaginary, accidental, or on purpose, just know it's a trap, and you're not going to take the bait! Say, "I'm not going to take it." Ephesians 4:31 in the Amplified Bible says, *"Let all bitterness and indignation and wrath [passion, rage, bad temper] and resentment [anger, animosity] and quarreling [brawling, clamor, contention] and slander [evil-speaking, abusive or blasphemous language] be banished from you, with all malice [spite, ill will, or baseness of any kind]."* Banish any kind of it and do not let it in!

When they're offended what do most people do? They spread it. The Bible puts gossipers and backbiters in the same category with murderers, fornicators, and homosexuals.

I learned a valuable lesson years ago when the Lord spoke to me on this. Tiz and I had been pastoring for some time, yet we never saw the blessings we knew had been promised to us. We didn't smoke, we didn't drink, we didn't go on vacation, but we never saw the blessing of God. We witnessed and we weren't just in prayer meeting once a week — we were in prayer meeting seven days a week, and then again at night! Still we did not see the full blessing of God. So I asked God why. My interpretation of James 1:5 is, "If any of you lack wisdom, let him ask God why." I explained to Him that we were laboring hard and doing all the right things. I mean we're holy!

Now God will always answer an honest question from an honest heart. I didn't know what was blocking the blessing. He said, "Yeah, you work hard, but you're mean, and you can't be a mean Christian."

Some of us come to church and say, "I love you, Lord," yet we hate our neighbor. We do it all the time! Do you tell others about Jesus Christ your Lord and Savior, but kill your pastor with your tongue in the next breath? In both 2 Chronicles 16:22 and Psalm 105:15, the Bible says, *"Do not touch My anointed ones."* We need to understand that goes beyond the pulpit. The person next to you is anointed. In answer to my question, God went on to say, "You've been planting seed, but you never get ahead, I'm making sure you don't. I'm killing your seed." Now, I love myself enough to say, "I better straighten up and do what is right."

The Bible says to put away all slander, evil speaking, brawling, contentions, animosity, resentment, and language. Banish it! Banishing something is more forceful than just getting rid of it. Throw it out of your life and change the locks on the door! Don't ever open that door again. If you really think about it, what gossip can possibly be worth keeping you out of the blessings of God? Who do you want to slander so badly that it becomes more important to you than the fulfillment of your divine destiny?

Being kind to one another is a decision. It's a choice. When we as a church start loving one another, church growth will explode worldwide! There won't be buildings large enough to hold us. God will draw them in from the north, the south, the east, and the west, and they'll be drawn to a family that has no discord.

Will offenses come? I guarantee it! It's impossible that they won't. Our response to those offenses determines the fulfillment of our destiny. The Bible says if any two agree together on earth it shall be done. So, let's agree right now that we're not going to receive or accept any offenses. We're going to love one another. We're going to be kind to one another. We're going to be gracious to one another, and we are going to be ready for an outpouring of His Spirit that goes beyond anything the church has ever experienced. Hallelujah!!

CHAPTER 2
DON'T TAKE IT!

At the beginning of Chapter 1, we began to look at the spirit of offense that has been released as a sign of the end of time. Let's look at it a little further. In Matthew 24, Jesus goes on to tell the disciples that the love of God is growing cold in the body of Christ. After His resurrection, Jesus asked Peter, "Do you love Me?" (John 21:15-17) Three times He asked the question, "Do you love Me no matter what?" That's really what it means. "Do you love Me no matter what? Do you AGAPE Me?" He says the love of many in the body of Christ will grow cold, because we have become self-centered. When we choose to take offense, we become "me" oriented. I thank God even though I offended Him before I was saved, and have offended Him even after, He still loves me unconditionally. This is what Jesus is saying to you. Will you love Me?

Three Types of Offenses

Let's look three types of offenses that exist in the world. The first are *imaginary offenses*. These are offenses that are real to you, but did not actually happen.

The second are *accidental offenses*. These are offenses where people said something or did something that really

25

offended you, but they didn't even know they were offending you. It was a real offense, but the other person was completely innocent. For example, people have said around me at times, "Well you got to 'Jew' the salesman down when you're buying a car." As a Jew, I could choose to take offense, but I know they don't mean anything by it and I'm not going to be offended. I ignore it.

The last type of offense is a *real offense* that is said with the sole purpose of being offensive. Example: You're walking down the road and someone yells a racial slur directed at you or somebody directs an insult at how you look. They mean to offend you. They wanted to offend you. If you take that offense, they got you.

Years ago Tiz and I pastored in Australia. We were there for almost six years and at that time, to be real honest with you, a lot of Australians did not like Americans. People would walk up to us in a restaurant and say, "What are you yanks doing here?" You know, making the choice to not be offended was a continual moment-by-moment battle.

Do you realize that every one of us is insecure in one way or another? The more insecure you are, the easier it is for you to be offended. If you've been offended, that means somebody tried to give you something and you took it.

Some friends of ours were getting ready to pioneer a church in Australia, and, since Tiz and I had lived there for a few years, we knew the people had a hard time with Americans. An Australian woman walked over to our friend while she was holding her new baby, looked at that baby and said, "That's a funny little dummy you got there." Our friend's wife just burst into tears! She told her husband, "I'm never going back to the church." For months it was an uphill battle. But it was an accidental offense, because in Australia a pacifier is called a "dummy". The lady wasn't pointing at her baby and saying, "That's a funny-looking little dummy you got there." She was pointing at the pacifier, but this lady took offense and it devastated her life for months until one day the lady came up and grabbed the pacifier and said, "You have to tell me where I can get one of these dummies." On a side note, the two ladies ended up being best friends!

So, there are imaginary offenses. There are accidental offenses. There are real offenses. No matter what form the bait takes, *we are not to take it.* Don't take it.

In Luke 17:1-2, Jesus says, *"'It is impossible that no offenses should come, but woe to him through whom they do come! It would be better for him if a millstone were hung around his neck, and he were thrown into the sea, than that he should offend one of these little ones.'"* The Bible is careful to spell it out for us: watch out that you don't spread offenses.

We also need to be cautious that somebody who's taken offense doesn't come and spread it to you. Words kill or words bring life. I recently read that an atom is the most powerful thing in the universe and you can't even see it. An atom configured a certain way can blow up everything around it. Scientists have divided the atom to see what causes it to be so powerful. When they finally divided it to its very core, you know what they found? Sound! Sound is what made it so powerful. God created the world with sound. Words! Words give life or death. Woe unto those who use words to spread offense, because they're killing people and killing their own destiny.

One thing I'm very careful about now is the people with whom I surround myself. The reason is because I protect my mind from anybody who will try to put destructive or negative thoughts in my spirit. If you're positive and speak faith then we have something to talk about because those words bring life. If you go around spreading offense, woe unto you!

The scripture says it's impossible to breathe and not be offended. Jesus said it's impossible. As long as you're around other people, you're going to be offended. It's going to happen. It is not a matter of if it will happen, it's a matter of what you do when it does happen. Will you take that offense? Will you take that curse and nurse it, feed it, grow it, spread it and pass it on? Or, will you say, "You know, what, thank you for that offense, but I won't take it!" It's going to happen, because we're real people. Whether imaginary offenses, accidental offenses or real offenses, you will encounter them all!

Why Avoid the Bait?

Now, why should we not take offenses? The word *offense* in the Greek is the word SKANDALON, where we get the word *scandal*. It means, "bait for the trap or snare."

God has a destiny for all of us; spiritually, in our families and financially. It is exceedingly and abundantly above anything we can ask or think, but we'll only fulfill it if we don't take offense. It's the bait in the trap. Don't take the bait. If Jesus doesn't come this week, you will have a prime opportunity to be offended; in your work, at home, in your marriage, in the church, wherever it is, there's a prime opportunity to be offended. Remember that offenses will come, but the reason they come is to trap you. What's the trap for? It's to keep you from your destiny. It's a trap to keep you from your blessing. It's a trap to keep you from being lifted up.

The Bible is full of men and women who walked into their destiny and men and women who missed their destiny. Everybody knows the story of Cain and Abel, but let's take another look at the story. I want to show you something. Genesis 4 tells us, *"Now Adam knew Eve his wife, and she conceived and bore Cain, and said, 'I have acquired a man from the LORD.' Then she bore again, this time his brother Abel. Now Abel was a keeper of sheep, but Cain was a tiller of the ground. And in the process of time it came to pass that Cain brought an offering of the fruit of the ground to the LORD. Abel also brought of the firstborn of his flock and of their fat. And the LORD respected* [received] *Abel and his offering, but He did not respect* [receive] *Cain and his offering. And Cain was very angry, and his countenance fell."* In other words, Cain was offended.

Cain and Abel were both raised by mom and dad to bring an offering to God. It had to be a blood offering. He knew that, but instead he said, "I'm going to bring what I've worked for, what I've tilled and grown. I'm not going to do it God's way, I'm going to do my way.", and God said, "I'm sorry, but I won't take it." He was offended at God, and the Bible says his countenance fell. His lip was sticking out. He was having a "poor me" day.

Verse 6 says, *"So the LORD said to Cain, 'Why are you angry? And why has your countenance fallen? If you do well, will you not be accepted? And if you do not do well, sin lies at the door. And its desire is for you, but you should rule over it.'"*

Now look at that. Sin lies at the door. Look at this in the Amplified Bible. It says, *"If you do well, will you not be accepted? And if you do not do well, sin crouches at your door; its desire is for you, but you must master it."* The trap is waiting. That offense is waiting for you to open the door. If you're offended, you open the door and it jumps on you. Remember, Satan is a roaring lion looking for somebody he can pounce on. So if you're offended, he pounces on you. Then it goes on to say that you've got to master being offended.

Let's look at the next verse. Verse 8 says, *"Now Cain talked with Abel his brother; and it came to pass, when they were in the field, that Cain rose up against Abel his brother and killed him."* Now here's human nature. God's dealing with Cain, but instead of going to God, he goes to Abel. I'm thinking that Cain said to Abel, "How come you're getting blessed and I'm not?" Abel must have said something like, "Well, Cain you know what to do. You know what's right." That created the offense. Cain took the offense and it turned into anger, which then turned into the very first murder in the human race.

He should have never gone to Abel. He should have gone to God and said, "God, what do I need to do to get this right?" But human nature doesn't want to go to God because God doesn't mince words. God tells us what we need to know, but we have to find somebody who will agree with us, and if they won't agree with us, then offense is multiplied to that person. God told Cain, "This offense is waiting to jump on you, and its desire is to master you, but you must master it." Take no offense that anybody offers you. You can't be offended unless you take it.

In Acts 24:16, Paul says, *"I myself always strive to have a conscience without offense toward God and men."* In Genesis 4:6, God is telling us that offense is waiting to jump on us. Like Paul, we must strive! Don't take the bait! Master that thing so it doesn't master us. We have to beat it, or it will beat us.

Paul says, "I exercise myself daily not to be offended." You know it's easy to say, "I want to be rich", but I found out you have to go out and do something before rich happens. It's easy to say, "I won't be offended.", but you have to work at it. It's hard work not to take offense!

We are all insecure to a certain degree. If somebody says something or somebody doesn't say anything, we take offense. If somebody says to you, "How are you doing?" Do you think to yourself, "What do you mean by that? What do you mean how am I doing? Don't I look like I am doing well?" If nobody says anything to you, do you think, "How come you didn't say anything to me? Don't you care how I'm doing?" Does any of this sound familiar? Am I making sense to you? If you're offended, it is because you chose to take the offense.

If we find somebody passed out drunk in the gutter, that person is not going to say, "I didn't want to drink. I was walking down the road and it jumped on me." or if man tells his son, "That river is dangerous, don't swim in that river. If you swim in that river, I'm going to spank your backside." The boy says, "Okay, daddy." The next day the dad takes the long way home by the river, and there is his son in the river. The Dad is standing there, and the son looks up and says, "Dad I didn't mean it." The dad says, "If you didn't mean it, then why did you bring your trunks?"

Ephesians 4 says when you are angry, don't sin. Don't let your wrath, fury or your indignation last until the sun goes down. Leave no room or foothold for the devil. Don't give him an opportunity. If somebody offends you, and you don't deal with it and get rid of it before the sun goes down, that thing is going to grow. It's going to multiply. It's going to spread. When you've taken offense, whether it be imaginary, accidental, or real, you've taken the bait the devil laid out for you.

I was recently told how people catch monkeys in South America. A person takes a coconut and cuts a small hole in it and inserts a shiny object in the hole. The monkey in curiosity reaches in to grab the shiny object, but can't pull his hand out because he has a tight fist wrapped around it and won't let go. Then the people walk right up and capture him. All that monkey has to do is let go of the shiny object, but because he's got his fist around it, he's trapped.

How many times are we like those monkeys? All we have to do is let go of the bait. But we don't want to, we won't let go of that offense. We won't let go of that racial statement. We won't let go of that statement our spouse made. We say, "I like my little offense. It's my offense."

Don't take offense and give foothold to the devil. If you have an offense, it's going to grow and it's going to spread. Every one of us is going to have an opportunity this week to be offended....and next week... and the week after... and the week after... Some may say, "Well, I'm just going to move to another city." Well, you can't run from your problem, because whereever you go, you'll take yourself along. I was listening to a preacher not long ago and he made a statement that is so very true. He said, "Offense is either going to make you bitter or make you better."

Matthew 5:22 says, *"But I say to you that whoever is angry with his brother without a cause shall be in danger of the judgment."* In many of your Bibles, if you look at the words, *without cause,* it's either in parentheses or it's italicized. Whenever you see that in the Bible understand that it's not in the original text. Man put it in there. Well, anybody who's been offended thinks they have a cause. They think, "Well, I have a right to be offended." But that's not what it says. It says whoever is angry with a brother or a sister *period.* There are no justifying phrases in the original text. There are no exceptions.

1 John 3:15 makes it very clear: *"Whoever hates his brother is a murderer."* In other words, anyone who is so much as angry with a brother or sister is guilty of murder. The simple moral fact is that words kill. Some of you tithe and give, yet God stops everything you touch. Are you gossiping or have you taken offense? He will stop your blessing. This is powerful. Jesus said, *"Father forgive them, they don't know what they are doing."* He would not take offense.

Proverbs 18:21 tells us that *"Death and life are in the power of the tongue."* Words kill. Watch what you say in fellowship. Watch what you say to your family. Watch what gates you open. Watch what atom bombs you release in the spirit of your minds.

Look at what Jesus had to say on the subject: *"This is how I want you to conduct yourself in these matters. If you enter your place of worship and, about to make an offering, you suddenly remember a grudge a friend has against you, abandon your offering, leave immediately, go to this friend and make things right. Then and only then, come back and work things out with God.*

"Or say you're out on the street and an old enemy accosts you. Don't lose a minute. Make the first move; make things right with him. After all, if you leave the first move to him, knowing his track record, you're likely to end up in court, maybe even jail. If that happens, you won't get out without a stiff fine." (Matthew 5:23-25 THE MESSAGE BIBLE) What "matters" is He talking about? Well, we just looked at Matthew 5:22 *"Whoever is angry at his brother."* He is talking about being angry because of an offense.

You might say, "But he offended me." Don't take it! Reverse it by doing something good. If you take offense, and you don't deal with it before the sun goes down, you will surely end up paying a stiff fine.

I was watching Charles Stanley not long ago and he was talking about how people had attacked him and offended him when he was first starting to build the church. He said people were trying to run him out of town. Then this little elderly lady invited him to her house and he went reluctantly. As he sat with her, she brought out a picture of Daniel and in this case the lions were behind him. Daniel was staring out the window and the sun was beaming down. Not only were the lions were behind him, but there were also the old bones of those who had already been eaten by them.

This old lady said, "Pastor, what do you see in that picture?"

He said, "Well, I see Daniel, lions, bones, and the light."

She said, "You're not seeing what God is saying." She tells him to look again.

He looks again and says, "Well, Daniel's hands are behind him, and she says, "No, let me show you what you should see in that picture."

Charles Stanley said the greatest sermon he had ever heard in his life was this one-liner from a little old lady! She said, "Pastor, the devil put those lions there to devour Daniel, but look at him. He refuses to look at the lions. He keeps his eyes on the Savior. The lions, bones, danger, pain, ridicule and the offenses are all behind him. Daniel refuses to look at the problems, but keeps his eye on the answer."

Isn't that powerful? When somebody wants to offend you, refuse to look at it. Refuse to take it! Keep your eyes on the Savior.

God has a marvelous destiny for you. Look at Moses. None of us will ever compare with what Moses accomplished, yet he got angry and it kept him out of the full blessing of God. Don't let that trap of anger keep you from your promised land blessing. Don't be offended. Don't take the bait!

There will always be imaginary offenses that seem very real. There will always be accidental offenses that still hurt. There are intentional offenses that wound deeply. Don't put it off any longer. Make a conscious decision to get rid of those offenses. God will do a miracle this very moment in your life.

Tiz and I have witnessed countless people with whom we have prayed be set free when they simply let go of offenses that they were holding onto. It may have been 50 years ago. It may have been five days ago. It may have been a husband, a wife, a church, a pastor, a stranger, a business partner, but today you're going to give it right back to the devil and take the blessing in its place.

Would you say, "Pastor Larry, I've battled with the pain of being offended and I want it broken right now?" For many of you the devil has all but killed your dreams and destiny because he laid a trap of offense. Today it can be broken and you can shut the door to that offense, and be put right back on a path of a wonderful destiny that God has always had for you. Get ready to reverse that curse and see the blessing of God come into your life. Say this out loud, "Father, I thank you today that offenses are broken off of my life. Forgive me for holding onto them. I release that person. I release myself. Every offense that ever came against me is broken and I send it away. Never again, will I take offense. Devil, you can try to give it to me. You can try to bring it to my house, my job, my church... Go ahead and bring it, but I won't take it! I will never again take offense, because you cannot stop my blessing. Starting today, I'm on a one-way journey right into the promised land in every area of my life in Jesus name. Amen!"

Chapter 3
Insecurity: a Result of Offense

One of the primary results of offense is insecurity. The moment we choose to take offense, our focus shifts from our destiny to ourselves. We become very self-centered. Our attitude says, "I don't care about my spouse, my kids, my job, or the body of Christ. All I care about is me and I have been offended!"

I want to show you how a man lost the destiny God had for him by simply letting insecurity take over his life. The word of God says in I Samuel 18, *"So David went out wherever Saul sent him, and behaved wisely. And Saul set him over the men of war, and he was accepted in the sight of all the people and also in the sight of Saul's servants. Now it had happened as they were coming home, when David was returning from the slaughter of the Philistine, that the women had come out of all the cities of Israel, singing and dancing, to meet King Saul, with tambourines, with joy, and with musical instruments. So the women sang as they danced, and said:*

'Saul has slain his thousands,

And David his ten thousands.'

Then Saul was very angry, and the saying displeased him; and he said, "They have ascribed to David ten thousands, and to me they have ascribed only thousands. Now what more can he have but the kingdom?"

Now I want you to see what's happening here. David has just saved Israel. The power and blessing of God is there, but because of offense and anger, Saul has become insecure and his destiny has changed forever. Instead of going down a glorious road that God had planned for him, he started going down the road of self destruction.

As we have already seen, we will all be offended at some time. Somebody is going to offend you at some point in your Christian walk. When you collect these offenses it's going to change you from a person who is secure in the destiny of God to a person of insecurity — and that insecurity doesn't stop; it grows and multiplies in your life.

Three Signs of Insecurity

There are three things that are signs of growing insecurity when we become offense collectors.

1 We become jealous.

Why am I jealous of somebody on television or somebody that has a better house? **When you see somebody who is blessed, and are jealous of that person, it's because you don't feel they are as worthy of the blessings of God as you are.** We are never jealous of somebody who is under us or behind us. We're only jealous of somebody who has something better than we do or somebody

INSECURITY: A RESULT OF OFFENSE

more recognized than we are. So when we're jealous, it's because we really don't believe they are as worthy of God's blessing as we are.

Think again of the Saul's story. He is king over the victorious nation. Israel has won the battle. Glory has been restored to the Israelites by the hand of a little shepherd boy. It's a blessing to Saul's kingdom, as well as to David.

So the victorious army comes home. Everyone is dancing in the streets and the women begin to sing. The first verse says "Saul has killed his thousands." Saul is feeling good. "Oh yeah! I'm the one! I'm the king!" But then the women sing the second verse, "And David has killed his tens of thousands!" What does Saul do? He could have said, "That's right! I've killed thousands. I've done great things for God and David is the next generation doing even greater things!" Instead, he chose to take offense. He becomes jealous at the praises that David is getting for the victory and of the hand God has on his life.

Jealousy is nothing more than a sign that we're insecure. When we feel jealousy it's because we have become an offense collector.

In Matthew chapter 20, Jesus tells a parable of some workmen. He tells of how the master comes to the job corps and hires some people and says, "If you'll come and work in the field for me, I'll give you a dollar a day." So the people are out there working and then noon comes, and the master goes back and finds some other people and says, "You know what? Come on in and work for me." Then at the last hour, he hires some more people for one hour. At the end of the day the master (who represents God), pays the ones who worked an hour first and he gives them a dollar. Then he pays the one who started at noon a dollar also. Well, the guys who worked all day are thinking they're going to get more, but he gives them a dollar. The Bible says they were upset.

Now watch this. They weren't upset because they felt ripped off. He had paid them the agreed wage. That's what the master said he'd do for them. They were upset because somebody else got as much as they did. Now isn't that human nature?

Then the master says, "Why are you upset? Why are you upset because I'm generous?" This is the way life is. We get a job, and they say, "We're going to pay you "x" dollars for that job, and then somebody else gets a raise, or somebody else gets a bonus and instead of being happy for that person, we become upset or jealous of that person's blessing. All it does is change our character.

Do you remember when Jesus was with Peter after His resurrection? He said, "Peter, do you love me?" Peter says, "Lord, you know I love you." He repeats it three times. We know the whole scenario. Then Jesus says to Peter, "Peter when you were young, you went wherever you wanted to go and did whatever you wanted to do, but there's going to come a time that you're going to have to pay a price for this." And Peter says, "What about John?" Now, Jesus isn't even talking to or about John. But Peter is saying , "I have to pay a price?? Does John have to pay a price, too? I don't mind paying a price if John has to suffer also."

That's insecurity. "Well, I don't mind paying the price if they have to pay, too." That is a sign that we're insecure.

We need to be secure in the fact that we are the children of God and never be jealous of somebody else's blessing.

"Well, I've been singing in the choir for 10 years now. How come I don't get to sing a solo?" Well, did you sing in the choir to lead people into worship or to be noticed? If your initial motive was right, why would you be jealous if somebody who is new in the choir comes up and sings a solo?

2 *We build walls.*

The second sign of insecurity is that we build walls up around us. Proverbs 18:19 in the Amplified Bible says, "*A brother offended is harder to be won over than a strong city, and [their] contentions separate them like the bars of a castle.*"

When we experience the insecurity that comes from being an offense collector, we put up a wall around ourselves. That wall is a "Catch 22." We're sending a signal that says, "You're not paying enough attention to me." So someone sees the signal and tries to pay attention to us, but the wall is in the way. We are so fortressed behind our wall that we can't be reached.

When we put these walls up around us, it's hard to let people break through. Saul was like this. What most people do not realize is that this is a spirit. The Bible tells us that in the beginning of their relationship, Saul loved David. After the spirit of insecurity entered the relationship, when the Spirit of God would touch Saul, he would cry out and say "David, my son!" Then five minutes later, he says, "I'm going to kill him!"

Now the women's song wasn't saying, "Up with David, down with Saul." But that is what Saul heard. That's what we think when we're insecure. The women were just saying that David has done a great thing, but Saul only heard ridicule.

Watch for those walls. We come to church and say, "I dare anybody to pay attention to me. I dare them." What we're really doing is saying, "Please, somebody pay attention to me." When I was a young convert and I'd get mad at the pastor, I'd move to the back row because I was letting him know something was wrong. Maybe your wall looks different. Maybe you don't go to church to get back at the preacher or leave out the tithes for a month. No matter how your wall looks, it is insecurity because you chose to take offense.

3 *We become critical.*

The third sign of insecurity is that we become critical of everybody and everything around us. Now I don't know that what I'm about to tell you is in the Bible, but I know that Saul thought the same way that you and I think. I can picture Saul sitting around with his buddies, discussing the women's song. Can you see Saul with his little gossip group saying, "Yeah, David had five stones and only one giant. Where was David's faith?" Do you follow me? "Oh, yeah, if he was such a man of God how come he needed five stones?" Of course, he carefully avoided the subject of Goliath's four other brothers, or the accuracy of the song.

The reason Saul chased David was to kill him so he wouldn't become king. He was determined to use his sword to stop the blessing of God in David's life, but David became king anyway. The only blessings stopped by Saul's sword were his own.

We have a sword in our mouth and we harm ourselves and others with our tongue. It's the devil's way of stopping God's blessing. Learn from Saul. The only blessings your sword will stop are your own.

Picture this with me; Goliath walks out in that field for day's challenging of the army of Israel. Now here are all the soldiers: the Green Berets, the Rangers, and the Seals. All the warriors are there. Here comes little David bringing his brother some lunch and he happens to get there about the time Goliath is cursing God and all of Israel. Israel and its best warriors have had days to go out there and fight. David walks into camp and says, "Why are you letting this uncircumcised Philistine talk to you like that?" Now the soldiers are saying, "Who do you think you are?" That's what they were saying to David. David responds, "It's not me, it's God, and somebody has to shut this guy up!" Instead of saying, "Yeah, David go get him," they criticized him for wanting to go and fight the battle. Why? Because they knew they were supposed to be doing it! A critical spirit stems from jealousy and a basic lack of security.

When we're insecure, what we really want to do is stop what God is doing in someone else's life. Remember when Joseph came and said to his brothers, "Guys I had a dream. I had a vision. I saw a coat of many colors." What did the brothers do? Instead of saying, "Oh man, God's really going to use you," they grabbed him, beat him up, tried to kill him, and threw him in a pit. When they got home, their father said, "Where's your brother?" They lied, "We don't know."

I wonder how many people we have tried to kill and throw into the pit through our spirit of criticism, because we have been jealous. There's no reason to be jealous or insecure because God is no respecter of persons. If He does something for somebody next to you, it just means He is getting ready to bless you!

As I was reading and praying over this, God showed me that this spirit of criticism, jealousy and insecurity in Saul not only ruined his own destiny, but was also passed down from generation to generation because he wouldn't deal with it. I have come to find, if mom's negative; daughters tend to be negative. If dad's negative; sons tend to be negative.

Saul needed Goliath killed so badly that he said, "The family of the one who kills this giant will never have to pay taxes again. You will inherit a large portion of the kingdom and you get to marry my daughter." That is how desperately he needed the enemy killed. So here comes the guy who killed the enemy and the very guy who wanted the enemy killed is now trying to kill the one who killed the enemy! Got that?

So David married Saul's daughter. In 2 Samuel 6:15-16, we see Saul's critical spirit reproduced in his daughter, *"So David and all the house of Israel brought up the ark of the LORD with shouting and with the sound of the trumpet.*

"Now as the ark of the LORD came into the City of David, Michal, Saul's daughter, looked through a window and saw King David leaping and whirling before the LORD; and she

despised him in her heart." David is excited because the presence of God is coming back to Israel.

In order to fully understand why David was so excited about the Ark of the Covenant's arrival in Jerusalem, we need to look at the whole story. After the defeat of the Philistines, the Ark of the Lord was being brought from the house of Abinadab where it had been kept. Look at what happened.

"And when they came to Nacon's threshing floor, Uzzah put out his hand to the ark of God and took hold of it, for the oxen stumbled and shook it. And the anger of the Lord was kindled against Uzzah; and God smote him there for touching the ark, and he died there by the ark of God.

"David was grieved and offended because the Lord had broken forth upon Uzzah, and that place is called Perez-uzzah [the breaking forth upon Uzzah] to this day.

"David was afraid of the Lord that day and said, How can the ark of the Lord come to me?

"So David was not willing to take the ark of the Lord to him into the City of David; but he took it aside into the house of Obed-edom the Gittite." (2 Samuel 6:6-10 AMP).

Now understand this, David had been offended by God and when David was offended by God, the presence of God was not in his life. Now they're bringing the Ark of the Covenant, or the presence of God back where it belonged. The presence of God comes back into your life when you stop taking offense. When you're offended, the presence of God is not there.

How many of you have ever sinned since you've become a Christian? How many want God to forgive you? Matthew 6:12 and 15 can easily be paraphrased to read, "And forgive us our offenses on the condition that we forgive those who have offended us. For if we do not forgive those who have offended us, God will not forgive us!"

So when you're offended and you hold and collect offenses, the presence of God is not there. It doesn't mean you're not saved. The presence of God is just not in your life. Learn from David. He finally got his heart right and decided not to be offended.

Going back to the story, David has repented for being offended and now the presence of God is coming back. He's excited and he's going ahead of the returning presence of God, dancing and rejoicing in the street. But now Saul's daughter is offended because David is happy. Sounds like church!

Look at again. In 2 Samuel chapter 6 it says, "*Now as the ark of the LORD came into the City of David, Michal, Saul's daughter, looked through a window and saw King David leaping and whirling before the LORD; and she despised him in her heart. So they brought the ark of the LORD, and set it in its place in the midst of the tabernacle that David had erected for it. Then David offered burnt offerings and peace offerings before the LORD.*"

Going on to verse 20: "*Then David returned to bless his household. And Michal the daughter of Saul came out to meet David, and said, 'How glorious was the king of Israel today, uncovering himself today in the eyes of the maids of his servants, as one of the base fellows shamelessly uncovers himself!'*"

46

Now I can't prove this by scripture, but I know this by human nature; if Micah is saying this to her husband, she first said it to the people around her. "Look at him. Who does he think he is? He's embarrassing me." You know before wives say it to husbands or husbands say it to wives, they usually say it to somebody else.

"So David said to Michal, 'It was before the LORD, who chose me instead of your father and all his house, to appoint me ruler over the people of the LORD, over Israel. Therefore I will play music before the LORD. And I will be even more undignified than this, and will be humble in my own sight. But as for the maidservants of whom you have spoken, by them I will be held in honor.'

"Therefore Michal the daughter of Saul had no children to the day of her death." (2 Samuel 6:21-23).

There are two ways to look at this. First, she was offended because her husband was an embarrassment to her and secondly, she may have been offended because David had the presence of God in his life, and her father had lost it. So she's jealous. Who knows why, but that offense was offered to her and she took it. The Bible says from that day on, she became barren.

One of the things God wants is for us to be fruitful and multiply. When we take offense, we become barren. We can become barren spiritually, financially, in relation with other people or in our relationship with God. Whatever it is, when we take on this character, which is not the nature of God, we become barren in one way or in many ways.

Why did she become barren? Well, maybe she was cursed by God, because she took offense. Maybe she became barren because she offended her husband, and her husband was repelled by her and was never with her again. We don't know how it played out, but we do know that because of taking this offense, she never fulfilled all that God had originally planned for her.

We'll look at this in more depth later in this book, but the Bible says where there is jealousy and envy, there is *every evil work*. So when we become offense collectors we become insecure. When we become insecure, instead of doing good, we become jealous, envious and critical Watch the domino effect that the devil has planned. Not only does it stop us from getting our blessing, but it opens the door for every evil work. That's heavy. Where there is jealousy and envy, there is an open door to every evil work.

Understand this; it's not up to you to stop the other person from offending you. The offense is offered to you by the devil so that you'll take the bait in the trap and effectively stop yourself from receiving your blessing.

Let look at one more scripture. This is so rich. In Haggai 1:5-7, the word of God says, *"Now therefore, thus says the LORD of hosts: 'Consider your ways! You have sown much, and bring in little; You eat, but do not have enough; You drink, but you are not filled with drink; You clothe yourselves, but no one is warm; And he who earns wages, earns wages to put into a bag with holes.' Thus says the LORD of hosts: 'Consider your ways!'"*

Here he says, "You're doing all the right things. You're giving; you're doing it but you're not getting ahead" You might be saying, "Well, I tithe. How come I don't get ahead?" or, "I give. How come I don't get blessed?"

Look at the scripture that goes along with what the Prophet Haggai said. Matthew 5:21-22 says, *"You have heard that it was said to those of old, 'You shall not murder, and whoever murders will be in danger of the judgment.' But I say to you that whoever is angry with his brother without a cause..."* Don't forget that *without cause* is italicized, which means man put it there. So, it actually says whoever is angry with his brother **period!** If you're angry, you've got a reason. Right? Someone said to me years ago, "All excuses are good excuses when they're your excuses." So man put that in there just to give us a way to slide out, but that's not what it says. It says, *"But I say to you that whoever is angry with his brother* [period] *shall be in danger of the judgment. And whoever says to his brother, 'Raca!' shall be in danger of the council. But whoever says, 'You fool!' shall be in danger of hell fire. Therefore if you bring your gift to the altar, and there remember that your brother has something against you, leave your gift there before the altar, and go your way. First be reconciled to your brother, and then come and offer your gift"*

Here's such a powerful understanding. You have a destiny in God that is absolutely phenomenal. It is exceedingly, abundantly above anything you could ask or think. But the number one bait in the trap is offense. Jesus is longsuffering, forgiving, patient and kind and does not render evil for evil. Jesus is not jealous. He's not envious. He is our example. So if we don't have the character of Christ, not only will God not allow us to be lifted up, but He'll have to hold us down because in this day and age people need to see Jesus in us.

Have there been holes in your bag? Have you been giving and not getting ahead? Now hear me. It's something everyone one of us has to exercise. Putting it in physical terms, you know the longer you don't exercise, the harder it is to get back in shape. The same is true with not taking offense. The longer you do not strive, or exercise, to keep from taking offense, the harder it is to be free, so you might as well start now.

Is there insecurity in your life? Is there jealousy? When you look at somebody and they're blessed or they get to sing and you don't or they come up with a new car and you think, "Man, I've been going to church as long as they have…" When you look at a situation like that, does it motivate or intimidate you? Are you critical? When you look at somebody, do you point at the answer or the problem? When somebody says, "That's a great business man", or, "That's a great business woman." do we respond by saying, "Yeah, but…" See, every one of us has the option of taking or leaving the bait. No one is exempt.

It's time to realize, if God will do it for somebody else, He's willing to do it for me! Even if God never does it for me, if it builds the kingdom of God and makes God's people happy, then glory to God! Isn't that the way we ought to be?

Maybe while you're reading this, the Lord is showing you areas in your life where you have been insecure or have held onto something that has bothered you for years and you have built a wall around yourself so that nothing can get in to hurt you. Pray this prayer, "Father, I come to You right now, in the name of Jesus. I know I've sinned. We've all sinned. But I know this; You love me so much You sent Jesus Christ to pay the price in full for all my sin. Right now, I receive Jesus Christ as my Lord and my Savior. Satan, I command you get out of my life, get out of my home, get out of family, get out of my mind, get out of my body, and get out of my spirit. I declare in the name, by the blood, through the power of the cross, I am born again; a child of God, totally forgiven, every curse, every family curse is broken and reversed. Forgiveness is mine. Joy is mine. Prosperity is mine. Health is mine. Freedom is mine. Dominion is mine. It's all mine. Not some day, but today! In Jesus' name. Amen and amen."

Chapter 4
Rage: The Silent Epidemic

Domestic violence: two words that describe a variety of crimes against men, women and children of all ethnic and social backgrounds. Perhaps domestic violence hasn't affected you or someone you know personally, so I will share a true story with you. My wife, Tiz, met a young woman at the mall when she was shopping one day. She was super-model beautiful and seemed to have everything going for her. Over time, Tiz built a friendship of trust with this young woman who finally started talking about how her husband would verbally abuse her. "If I try to leave he will physically abuse me. I know no man will ever want me! I'll never get married again, I am no good!" Her husband had her convinced that she was ugly and nobody else would want her. He had convinced her that she was lucky to have him.

In studying this, I have found that most women who are abused think they deserve it. Nobody deserves to be abused! Nobody has to take it. You don't have to take it. Whether it's physical abuse or verbal abuse or emotional abuse or sexual abuse. Men may hit more often with their hands and women may hit more often with their emotions. The whole reason is to control or dominate because of the presence of anger in that person's life.

Women are beaten severely every 15 seconds in America. The leading cause of injury to women between the ages of 15 and 24 is physical abuse. Medical expenses are astronomical because of domestic violence in America alone.

You don't deserve to be abused, you didn't cause the abuse, and you don't have to take it anymore!

There are so many different types of rage. It seems you hear about a new one every time you turn on the News. There is road rage, air rage, office rage, desk rage, work rage, bike rage and stalker rage. Remember, we're not just talking about men being angry, there are women and children who are angry too. The question is what is the source of this anger? Anger is the fruit, so we need to locate the root.

The Roots Of Anger

1 *Family Curses*

Society will tell you that most abusers were abused. We've been raised in that atmosphere. Dad was angry. Mom was angry. Grandpa and grandma were angry. Often we hide behind the excuse of "It is the Latino fire or the Irish fire". No, it's called a family curse. The Bible says the iniquity of the father or the mother is passed on to the third and the fourth generation.

How many times do we do or say something and hurt the ones we love most, then say, "Why am I like that? I'm never going to do that again!" We tell our spouse, "Honey I'm sorry. I'll never do that again. I promise you!" and we mean it with all of our hearts. There's something in us that makes us do what we don't want to do.

Why do people have rage? What makes a person with rage take their actions to the next level, acting on their emotions and committing horrific acts? Kip Kinkel shot 26 Thurston High School students in May of '98. Before that tragic day he wrote a letter to his Mom and said, "Mom I love you, but I can't help it." Then he walked up, shot and killed his mother.

We can see example after example of this. It seems nearly every week we hear of some new outbreak of killing rage because somebody has been offended. So they take a gun and start killing people. Nowhere is exempt. It happens in schools, at work, in malls, and in churches.

Look at yourself. Are you an angry man? Are you an angry woman? Are you full of rage? What makes you different from people who commit unspeakable crimes? You might immediately think your "temper" is nothing compared to what those gunmen have done, but remember what we've already seen... our words destroy.

You need to understand that anger can be explosive anger or it can be boiling anger. It can be hitting something or being depressed. It can be lashing out at someone else or even yourself. It could be hurting someone else or committing suicide. Anger shows up in all kinds of forms, but all you have to do is look at yourself. Look at what's happening in you and then go back and say, "Was this in mom? Was this in dad? Was this in grandma or grandpa or one of the other family members?"

We are just starting to realize these are not isolated incidents, but an epidemic we've been ashamed to talk about it. Anger can be in the form of envy or jealousy or depression.

Anger is not the primary, but a secondary emotion. Something has opened the door so that anger in any of these areas can affect us. For example, look at the roots of insecurity. Something from your past has made you feel insecure about yourself. Everyone feels insecure on some level. This insecurity causes us to take personally, anything that's said or done to us.

2 Frustration

We get angry when we feel frustrated or powerless or out of control in situations around us. Our response is to try to control the situation through anger and through violence.

3 Shame and embarrassment

If we feel embarrassed, we get angry. If we feel somebody has embarrassed us or somehow caused us to feel shame for some reason, it makes us feel threatened. We are then vulnerable and anger brings control and confidence back to our life.

4 Exhaustion

We get so tired that we feel we can't take it anymore. We start to get mad. If we walk around angry, it will build and build and build. When we start to feel that anger, it's lying at the door waiting to come in to ruin our life, but God said we can rule over it. "Well, I lost control." Stop losing it and start holding onto it!

How To Deal with Anger

1 *Confess it*

As we've already seen, if we are going to get rid of the spirit of anger, we must first acknowledge the problem and confess it. Don't you dare tell your wife or your husband, "If you go in for counseling, I'll beat you to a pulp!" Don't you dare. Don't ignore it. Ignoring a problem does not make it go away, it causes it go underground where it can grow and flourish. Do not ignore it. Admit it. Confess your faults one to another. Confess. Cain would not confess. When God said, "Where's your brother?" Cain responded, "Am I my brother's keeper?" And that family curse went all the way down to his grandson, Lamech. Lamech murdered a man because he said or did something to hurt him. Every commentary I've read concerning the story of Lamech says that when he tells his wife about it, he's not only bragging, he's writing a poem about it.

A society that ignores a problem for one generation will see the next generation embrace the problem. We're in a generation that embraces rage. This generation writes violent bumper stickers, video games, television and even cartoons showing violence. The generation before ignored it, now this generation is embracing it, and it is growing.

Iniquity does not just pass on to the next generation; it abounds and multiples, so now is the time to look at your children. Look at your dad. Now look at your kids. Are they hitting people?

Don't be fearful; be set free.

2 Deal with it positively

Deal with it, but deal with it positively. If you feel insecure, you're going to take everything as a threat. God says you need to go to the mirror (the Word of God) and see yourself the way God sees you. You're a winner not a loser. You're to be the head and not the tail. Remember that anger will not bring the blessing of God, so no matter what anybody said about you, get rid of it. Don't drag it around. Don't drag what some teacher said about you 35 years ago. Don't drag what some relative said about you. Don't drag that garbage around. Cut it loose. Quit looking back. Your harvest is not behind you; your harvest is in front of you. Repeat this, "I don't feel insecure anymore. Somebody loves me."

At the work place we have to be nice to everybody because we're doing business deals, but we feel frustrated. We come home and now we're back in the real world with our spouse and kids, and we let our anger explode. So what if you lose a business deal? Don't bring that anger and disappointment home.

Here's how you don't bring it home: if you lose a business deal, don't blame her, don't blame him, don't blame them, because number one it's the devil who stole your business deal. If you're mad at your spouse or kids, you don't know who the real thief is. If you know who the thief is, get mad at him. The Word of God promises that when the thief is caught he must repay what he stole, multiplied many times (Proverbs 6:31).

Let me give you the saying that launched me into faith. *"All things work together for good"* (Romans 8:28). All things work together for good. So if all things work together for good, why would you ever have a bad day? How can you be frustrated if you know that eventually everything is going to turn out right, even if it is not in the way or at the time you expected? It only turns out wrong when you get frustrated because you think it's not going to work.

3 *Dealing with embarrassment or shame*

What if something or somebody embarrasses you or puts shame on you? First you must realize that there is none righteous, no not one, and that includes you. So if you make a mistake, so what? If you feel threatened by a mistake or by embarrassment or by shame, reverse that by understanding that God has chosen the foolish to confound the wise. Don't take it personally. You can't control what happens to you, but you can control what happens in you.

4 *Dealing with exhaustion*

We get frustrated when we're exhausted. Here's the answer: Spend more time with God and more time with positive people.

Anger stops the blessing of God from being released into your life. God wants to do it, but an angry man or an angry woman will stop the blessing. Nobody, when they're a child says, you know what? When I grow up, I think I'll be a drug addict. You know, when I grow up, I think I'll be an alcoholic. Nobody does that on purpose.

Tiz is from Montana. I'm from south St. Louis. Two different worlds. When we got married, she found out she married somebody she didn't really know. And the real me would rise up. Now I would try to subdue my anger. But that's not the answer. We're not talking about controlling anger. There are a lot of books and things already out there about controlling anger. We don't want to control anger. We don't want to control alcoholism. We don't want to control drug addiction. We want to be set free, because whom the Son sets free is totally free.

So we bring our problems home from work. We bring our anger home. We come home; snorting and stamping around like a wild animal of some kind. Now it may take days or it may take weeks or it may take months, but eventually our family is walking on eggshells. The kids say, "Is Dad coming home?" or "What kind of mood is Mom in?" Their security is gone.

Early in Tiz and my marriage, I hit her. She was pregnant and I knocked her down the stairs. Now I'm not proud of the fact, but I'm telling you to make a point. I refused to go for help. It's a miracle of God that my wife stayed with me.

When we think of anger, we think of explosive anger. We think about road rage or office rage or air rage or desk rage or work rage or school rage or bike rage.

I remember on one trip to Vancouver, Washington, Tiz and I saw this guy riding a bike. Now, we don't normally think of bicycle riders as being filled with rage; after all, they should be working it off with all that pedaling — right? Well, this cyclist got so filled with rage at a man in a car who had not given him enough room, that at the next stop, he jumps off his bike, goes up to the car, reaches in through the window and starts bashing the driver! See what I mean? Rage robs you of good common sense!

We live in a society that has embraced the concept of anger. We have bumper stickers that are angry: "Hang up and drive!" "Mean people suck!" "The only way you'll get my gun is to pry it from my cold dead fingers." Society has embraced anger, but God has not. Anger is a spirit that always destroys.

Children hate their parents. Parents hate their parents. People hate you at work. You must destroy anger before anger destroys you, your marriage and your home. I'm going to show you how to *block* and *reverse* the root of your anger.

CHAPTER 5

BITTERNESS: THE ROOT OF ANGER

When a person has an angry spirit, God cannot do what He wants to do. One cause of cancer is a spirit of anger. Anger never releases the blessing of God. Instead, it always stops God from doing what He wants to do. Being an angry person doesn't necessarily mean you are hitting people or punching holes in the walls. There are other forms of anger. An angry person is nothing like Jesus, the Prince of Peace. Being a mean Christ-like person is like being a longhaired bald man, or a tall short man. It's impossible to be a both mean and Christ-like. John chapter 15 talks about an owner of a vineyard. In that chapter, we see God as the Owner and ourselves as the vines. So the Owner of the vineyard comes and looks among the vines. While He's walking around looking at His vines, He says, "Why is this one not bearing any fruit of the Spirit — love and joy and happiness and kindness and longsuffering and peace. It's dead weight," He says, "pull it out; get it out of here."

People who punch each other are not showing love. Gossipers, backbiters, and slanderers are always tearing people down. They never build anyone up or encourage them. God says when we take communion, this is why there are many weak and sick and dying among us. Why? Because we're not treating each other the way we ought to. This is why sickness is in the body of Christ. This is why there is divorce and lack; and so many other things that God hates: we don't treat the body of Christ the way Christ treats us.

Hebrews chapter 12, verse 14 says, *"Pursue* [go after] *peace with all people."* That ties directly into Matthew 5:9, *"Blessed are the peacemakers."* Now, all coins have a flip side, so if "blessed are the peacemakers," then flip that coin over and "cursed are the troublemakers." You may not be one of those who go around punching people, but you verbally kill people with your tongue.

Proverbs 6:16 tells it like it is: *"These six things the LORD hates, yes, seven are an abomination to Him ... one who sows discord among the brethren."* This may be in the family or in your marriage or in the body of Christ or in the work-place. Obviously this is not just, "Yeah; I ought to be a nice person." This is a matter of life and death to the things of God that He desires to do in you and through you.

"Pursue peace with all people, and holiness, without which no one will see the Lord." (Hebrews 12:14) Now, this does not mean we will not go to heaven if we do not pursue peace with all people. It just means we won't see the Lord in His blessing and in His anointing and in His outpouring of goodness. It puts peace and holiness in the same category. It puts being holy and being a nice guy in the same category.

Verse 15 of Hebrews 12 takes us another step: *"Looking carefully lest anyone fall short of the grace of God; lest any root of bitterness springing up cause trouble, and by this many become defiled. "* If we refuse to deal with being a mean person, it will begin to defile all those around us. If we still ignore it, eventually a root will spring up and move you out of the body of Christ. I meet Christians all the time who say they believe in God and they love God, but they don't go to church because of people. I can tell you that 99.99999% time of the time that person is a mean person.

We are inclined to think anything that is not violent or filled with rage is not anger. But God shows that somebody who is full of bitterness and anger is literally a mean person. Most people do not set out to be deliberately unkind, however, we need to face meanness and deal with it so Jesus can come and set us free.

Characteristics of a Mean or a Bitter Spirit

1 It's judgmental

It's amazing how a mean person sees the flaws in everyone but themselves.

2 It's rebellious

A mean person will not submit to authority because they want to be the authority. Rebellion is as the sin of witchcraft. A rebellious person will not submit to a spiritual covering. An uncovered person's mind is open to witchcraft. Crazy things and crazy thoughts become a reality in their mind.

3 It craves isolation

Mean or bitter people isolate themselves from the rest of society. In the Christian church, they isolate themselves from the body of Christ.

4 It hangs around with wrong people

Children who are angry will be drawn to the wrong friends. Like begets like.

5 It's stubborn

A person with a bitter or mean spirit will refuse to hear the other side of someone's story.

6 It's unthankful

They can never be thankful for what they have; they're always mad about what they don't have. They can never be thankful for what someone has done for them; they can only point out what has not been done for them.

7 It is sarcastic

A mean person takes jabs. For example, a husband will take public jabs at his wife and then laugh about it, as though it's humorous. When she says she's hurt, the husband will hide behind the nice-guy image and try to pass it off as a joke. But he wasn't joking — it was a jab.

Anger or bitterness is the fruit, but we need to look once again for its root. In the last chapter we examined the possibilities that it may be a family curse. Is anger or depression or bitterness a family curse? If it is, not only will it pass onto you, it will multiply, because iniquity doesn't just pass on; iniquity abounds, it grows. Look what has happened to our nation. Back in the sixties, if Ozzie and Harriet were ever seen in a bedroom, we saw twin beds with a nightstand in between them, and neither one of them ever touched the bed. Look what's on public television today! Iniquity does not just pass on; iniquity grows. So what was in grandpa and grandma grew to your dad. What was in your mom and dad grew to you. And what's in you will grow to your children. It will multiple and abound. But whom the Son sets free is free indeed (John 8:36), but we must be man enough or woman enough to say, "Yes, this is it." Confess. You can come to God with heroin; you can come to God with cocaine; you can come to God with adultery. There's only one thing you can't come to God with, and that's pride because pride won't let you come to God.

We've all heard people being described as a mean person or a bitter person. You can cut the fruit off a tree, but unless you kill the root, it's going to keep on growing.

Chapter 6
The Roots Of Bitterness: Jealousy and Envy

As I was doing this study, I was absolutely amazed at how many scriptures are in the word of God about jealousy and envy. Do you think jealousy and envy can really cause problems? It's the beginning of all problems! Satan looked at God and instead of saying, "You know what? I've got a good deal here." He said, "You know what? I want to be equal with God." And that jealousy, envy and bitterness were the root of Lucifer's problems, along with every problem that we see on the face of the earth today. Where there is jealousy and envy, there is the open door for every evil work.

Now, we don't like to admit this, but when we look at somebody who's being blessed; or somebody who can do something we can't; or think someone is smarter, taller, better looking or making more money or getting more fame than we are; what jealousy and envy really say is, "If I can't win, I don't want anyone else to win." If we allow that spirit of jealousy and envy to come in to our life, at that moment we begin to be a vessel of dishonor instead of honor. We begin to say things and do things to try to destroy others. But remember; what you sow is what you reap. (Galatians 6:7)

Two Forms of Jealousy and Envy

Number one: I didn't get what I deserve

Deal with that right now. I believe with all my heart that one of the reasons we're seeing such violence on our streets with our kids is because multiple generations have refused to get rid of that attitude. But here's the reality. If you get rid of it now, the master avenger is about to come and bring in not only the latter rain but also the former rain. What we should have had, we're going to get back. God wants to bless us and give us the desires of our hearts, but first we must get rid of jealousy and envy.

Number two: They got it, and they didn't deserve it.

We look at somebody and say, "You know what? Man, I work harder than they do. I do all this extra stuff and they got my promotion. I work and work to make ends meet and, I mean, they're crooks and look at how they prosper! " When you think that way, you are actually putting your judgment above God's.

Jealousy and envy is a destructive force. God blessed Abel and Cain became jealous. Hopefully, we would never even consider killing somebody, but jealousy and envy will cause us to verbally kill people. Why do you think the gossip columns are so big and popular? "So and So Movie Star had an affair with an alien." The reason we even read that stuff is because we want to hear something bad about someone we think is more blessed than we are because jealousy and envy says, "If I can pull that person down, it will make me feel higher." That is a root of bitterness. And hear me; it won't stop the blessing in anybody's life but yours. Every person has to deal with it, you have to choose daily to live as the Bible teaches.

If you feed jealousy and envy they will grow and win. If you're going to look at people, be motivated by their blessings instead of being intimidated or jealous. I like hanging around with people who do things better than I do. I am motivated by it, because I believe God is no respecter of persons. Whatever He has done for someone else, He will do for me. So I refuse to be intimated. I decide to be motivated.

An old Indian accepted Christ late in life. A few weeks later, a preacher asked him how he was doing. He said, "Well, I feel as though a black dog and a white dog were fighting inside me."

"Which one is winning?" asked the preacher.

The Indian replied, "Whichever one I feed."

Whichever dog you feed is going to win, but you are the person who has to decide which one to feed. If jealousy and envy enter in, and you allow that feeling to stay, the door is open for every evil work.

Numbers 5 calls it a spirit of jealousy. Proverbs 6:34 says, *"Jealousy is the rage of a man."* Psalm 79:5 says, *"How long will Your jealousy burn like a fire?"* Israel was devoured by the fire of His jealousy. Job 5:2 (KJV) says, *"Envy slayeth the silly one."* Proverbs 14:30 says, *"A sound heart is life to the body, but envy is rottenness to the bones."* Proverbs 27:4 (KJV) says, *"Wrath is cruel, and anger is outrageous; but who is able to stand before envy?"* Anger is bad. Wrath is bad, but nobody can stand before envy. Anger is bad, it will do you harm. Wrath is bad, it will do you harm. No one will be able to stand when they allow envy to come into their lives. Envy is an emotion. Anger is an emotion, but so is praise, so is joy, and so is happiness.

Envy caused the whole fall. Remember that scripture we read. It says it will defile many. Satan brought a third of the angels with him. Everyone who has this bitter spirit is going to try to get somebody to listen to them. It started the whole problem, but look what happened down the line. Matthew 27, verse 15. *"Now at the feast, the governor was accustomed to releasing to the multitude one prisoner whom they wished. And they had then a notorious prisoner called Barabas. Therefore, when they had gathered together, Pilate said to them, whom do you want me to release, Barabas or Jesus who is called Christ? For he knew that because of envy they had delivered him."* They killed Jesus because they were jealous, because people were following Him and they were afraid.

Every one of us has the ability to kill what God is doing in someone's life because of jealousy. The reality of it is whatever you try to kill; that thing is going to resurrect, and you're the one who will lose. I'm not writing this to you like someone who walks on water. I'm writing this as someone who realizes the truth of this, the revelation of this, and has to deal with this. I'm a real human being, and I realize that if I give in to envy and jealousy, I give place to the devil and will destroy the blessing God wants to bring into my life. It's something that every one of us has to deal with. The only reason we gossip and, talk against someone is to kill them. That's the only reason. We don't want them to win.

Romans 1 places envy and murder in the same category. Philippians 1:15 says, *"some preach Christ with envy and strife"*. Quit talking against this person and that person and this doctrine and that doctrine. Even preachers can preach Christ with envy and strife. You know how? By trying to tear that person down to build ourselves up. That is not the way Jesus did it. It's not Christ-like.

Jealousy and envy: each of us have to deal with it every day. If I don't deal with it, it will kill me. It will kill you. This is a spirit of jealousy and envy.

CHAPTER 7

THE ROOTS OF BITTERNESS: NOT FORGIVING OTHERS

The lack of forgiveness. I remember a precious lady Tiz and I met while we were preaching in Perth, Australia. This wonderful lady; you could see the holiness and the love of God in her life. She had been in the church for 40 or 50 years and was born and raised in church. She was about 60 years old, but she had a hip that was deteriorating. Three nights in a row she came up to be prayed for, but there was no outward sign of her healing.

On the fourth night we were praying for her and all of a sudden the Spirit of God impressed upon us to ask her if there was anybody her life she hadn't forgiven… anybody she was bitter against… anybody she was mad at? She said, "No, no, there's nobody." And yet we could tell there was something. So we asked again, "Is there anybody?" Suddenly she began to weep. About 40 years before this, her sister had married the man this woman loved. She had carried that bitterness with her for more than 40 years! We then prayed with her as she forgave her sister and repented of her sins.

When Jesus forgave you, He forgot it. The devil, who is the accuser of the brethren brings up the past. If you have forgiven, and you bring up the past with your husband, wife, or anyone else, you are actually moving aside the blood of Jesus and resurrecting something that He has forgotten. And we — you and I — become the accuser of the brethren.

Let me paraphrase the story we see in Matthew 6: The disciples came to Jesus and said, "Lord, when we pray nothing happens. When you pray blind eyes open; storms cease; gold coins come out of fishes' mouth. Teach us how to pray." So Jesus says, "Here's how you pray. When you pray say, 'Father. When you pray, praise My name. My Father, who art in heaven, hallowed is Your name. Your kingdom come, Your will be done, on earth as it is in heaven. Give us this day our daily bread. Forgive us our trespasses, on the condition that we forgive those who have trespassed against us. Lead us not into temptation, but deliver us from the evil one, for Yours is the kingdom and the power and the glory forever. For if you do not forgive those who have sinned against you, I will not forgive you.'" One time He goes through the entire prayer, but then He goes back to the area of forgiveness three more times.

If you dwell on or refuse to let go of the past, you have not forgiven. If you have not forgiven, then you cannot be forgiven. That does not mean you are not born again. Since you've been born again have you sinned? Do you want to be forgiven? The only thing that can keep us from our forgiveness is if we're not willing to forgive others.

How many times have you heard of "holding a grudge"? Here's a grudge. Somebody hands it to you and you hold it. Not only do you hold it, but you take it home with it. Not only do you take it home, but you feed it, you hold it close to your heart, nurse it, stroke it, and share it with others. Holding a grudge... holding it. Not only do we nurse it. We make sure that grudge stays alive and grows. If it looks sick we go to somebody else so that they can pray over it too and make sure that grudge is growing.

Like you, I've heard that terminology all my life, so I went to the Webster's Collegiate Dictionary to look up the word grudge. Here is what I found: A grudge is a "feeling of deep-seated resentment, wishing ill will and malice". So when we hold the grudge, it becomes deep-seated, way down in our personality. Right along with that grudge, we have malice toward the one who offended us. We want them to hurt. We want them to suffer pain. That is not Christ-like.

When you're a wounded person, not only do actual wounds grow, but imaginary wounds become real. You become a grudge collector. They become like Beanie Babies. Your house is full of them; your shelves are full of them. So how can we deal with this? The Bible says we battle not against flesh and blood. So if somebody wounds you, and you're mad at them and you hold onto anger and you nurse it and you feed it and you grow it and you want to give them a pay back, the Bible says you're fighting the wrong battle. You can't win. If you're holding a grudge, if you haven't forgiven somebody, you can't win. And the reason you can't win is you're fighting in the wrong battle because you're mad at a person. You've lost sight of your enemy.

Suppose you drive up to a construction site. A beautiful home has just been completed. Do you go to the tool box, find the hammer, and shower it with compliments, then ask it to come build your house? Or if someone picks up that hammer and knocks a big hole in the wall, do you punish the hammer and send it back to its toolbox? Of course not, a hammer is a tool. We are also tools. If we are building people up, we're in the hands of the Carpenter. If we're tearing people down, we're in the hands of the destroyer.

Let me ask you, whose hand were you in last night? Before you begin to talk about somebody else, stop and ask yourself, "Am I in the hand of the Jesus or in the hand of Satan?" You don't get mad at the hammer. You don't give the hammer glory. We do not battle against flesh and blood. You must understand who the thief is!

If you're still angry with the guy who divorced you or the woman who divorced you, then that grudge has you. The Bible says God has come to heal the brokenhearted. You can receive the grudge and the curse that comes with it, or you can let go of it when you realize that your battle is not against flesh and blood.

When Jesus hung on the cross, He said, "Father forgive them. They don't know what they're doing."

What did He mean, "They don't know what they are doing?" They plotted; they paid Judas off; they nailed Him to a tree; and they rigged the court. What did He mean? He understood the battle: they were hammers in the hands of the destroyer.

I believe that had Jesus given in to anger at that point and been mad at them, He would not have been able to be the unspotted Lamb of God and the plan of salvation would have failed. Thank God He stood firm!

In Ephesians 6:12, Paul makes sure we cannot misunderstand this very important key to forgiveness: *"For we do not wrestle against flesh and blood, but against principalities, against powers, against the rulers of the darkness of this age, against spiritual hosts of wickedness in the heavenly places."* In other words, it's not your spouse; it's not your kids; it's not any human being — it is the devil and his hosts of darkness. Once we have an understanding of this; that no person is our enemy; it will be much easier to forgive them before bitterness takes root. And when we catch the real enemy — the devil — he has to restore everything he has stolen from us... the marriage God intended for us to enjoy, the spiritual, physical, and financial blessings He wanted us to have.

Choosing to forgive others will always open the door, not only to our own forgiveness, but to all the blessings of God. Make that choice now and refuse to back down! Stand firm in your decision to forgive. I promise you won't regret it!

Chapter 8

The Roots of Bitterness: Not Forgiving Yourself

It is very important to remember that anger and bitterness do not only show themselves by lashing out at others. Sometimes it's lashing out at yourself. Sometimes it's anger and unforgiveness at yourself. There are a lot of people who have forgiven others, but they've never forgiven themselves and they can't receive the blessing of God because they don't believe they deserve it.

I remember a girl in one of the churches Tiz and I pastured. She was a great gal with a beautiful child, but Tiz and I noticed there was never any joy. I prayed, "God, what's wrong here?" The Lord told me, so I had Tiz get her and bring her back into my office. And I said, "Child, I'm going to ask you something, and if I'm wrong, tell me." I asked, " Were you ever a Lesbian?" When I said that to her, the water works came.

"Yes, I was, she responded. "I was so afraid somebody would find out."

I said, "You know what, child, nobody needs to find out. But there's One who knew all along; that's why He died on the cross."

Isaiah 1:18 says, "'Come now, and let us reason together,' says the LORD, 'Though your sins are like scarlet, They shall be as white as snow.'" The word scarlet means double-dyed; irremovable by any of man's washings. Though our sins are like scarlet, He'll make them whiter than snow. That means it's so deep — it's so way down in there that nothing man can do will remove that stain; but one touch of the Master's hand, and every sign of that stain is gone.

The Bible says all things work together for good. (Romans 8:28) God never made me a drug addict, but because of what I've gone through, I love all kinds of people. I can sit with governors or drug addicts. I can sit with businessmen or prostitutes. I can sit with dope dealers, inmates or college professors. They can tell me anything without shocking me — I've seen it all. Now God uses all those experiences so we can win the world to Jesus. Luke 7:47 says, "But to whom little is forgiven, the same loves little." The flip side of that coin is "He who has been forgiven of much, loves much." Whether you were a murderer or a gossiper, or you get your drugs from somebody in the streets or from the doctors with a prescription, or you were robbing banks or robbing your income tax, or whether you went to church all your life and did your best to "be good" — we all need Jesus.

In one of the churches Tiz and I pastored, there was a man who had spent 35 years in prison for killing the man who raped his sister. He had been sentenced to death. On the day of his execution, he was taken to the gas chamber. He was moments away from death when the phone rang and he was pardoned. Now, obviously I'm condensing his story a lot, but he got out of prison, got saved, baptized and delivered from the spirit of bitterness. He went on to become a key person in one of the cell groups in that church. And the focus of his ministry? Praying for other people who needed deliverance from the spirit of bitterness. God took all the horror he had been through and brought good out of it. Now others are being delivered from anger and bitterness because he understands and prays for them.

As we saw in the last chapter, you need to forgive people from your past. That goes hand-in-hand with forgiving yourself. Yes, what they did was real. Yes, it was probably wrong. Yes, it hurt, but Jesus has come to heal the brokenhearted. He'll turn your scars into stars. He'll turn your hurts into halos. Let go of it. Let go of it and realize who the enemy is. Once you clearly see the enemy, you win the battle. Not only that, but let's say you have carried this hurt for 20 years. Do you know that all the joy, all the happiness, all the blessing you should have had for 20 years, you get back? All the joy; all the blessing; all the goodness; the good marriage you should have had — you get it all back.

God knows what we did, that's why He sent a Savior. You think you have to pay the price, but the price has already been paid. Forgive yourself. Maybe you had an abortion, maybe you did other things you find hard to forgive, but forgive yourself anyway. "I'm not worthy," you say? You are so worthy that God Almighty sent His Son, the Lamb of God, for you. If He says you are worthy of forgiveness, who are you to argue with Him? You need to forgive yourself.

Chapter 9

The High Price of Anger

Years ago there was a television series on the Beach Boys. It showed how some of the Beach Boys got involved with the wrong crowd and became angry and disruptive. Then it showed that they had gotten this inheritance from their dad. One scene showed that both the grandfathers were also abusive toward their spouses and toward their children. This generational curse passed on from generation to generation.

Being angry doesn't mean you explode. You could be a quiet angry person. You could be an explosive angry person or a seething angry person. But anger will cost you.

In the documentary about the Beach Boys, you see the obvious fruits of the spirit of anger in these people's lives and what it cost them in their families and relationships. But one part really caught my attention. The dad was mad at the Boys and so he sold some of their song rights to get even with them. He sold those rights for $700,000. At the end of the program, the biographer said that what the dad sold in anger for $700,000, today is worth $75 million. So, even in the natural realm, there is a cost if we won't deal with the spirit that the Bible calls anger.

Before we leave this subject, let's look one more time at the story of Moses. The Bible says, *"Then the LORD spoke to Moses, saying, 'Take the rod; you and your brother Aaron gather the congregation together. Speak to the rock before their eyes, and it will yield its water; thus you shall bring water for them out of the rock, and give drink to the congregation and their animals.' So Moses took the rod from before the LORD as He commanded him. And Moses and Aaron gathered the assembly together before the rock; and he said to them, 'Hear now, you rebels! Must we bring water for you out of this rock?'"*

Notice Moses said, *"Hear now you rebels."* Every leader reading this book can understand his feelings at that moment. At some time or another we have all been tempted to just "let 'em have it," but we must get control of that anger. As we have already seen in this story of Moses, there is a high price to pay if we do not.

If we're angry people we will not receive what God desires to do in us, for us and through us. One of the reasons why the churches in America aren't seeing the miracles God has for them and why our divorce rate is as high as the secular rate is because we're angry at each other as denominations. We're angry at churches across the road. We won't work with other churches because they don't believe exactly like we do. We walk around with our holier-than-thou noses in the air and can't figure out why the unbelievers aren't coming to our church. We're angry at each other and gossiping and slandering or continually saying or thinking something evil about somebody.

Many people have taught that Moses never got to go into the promise of God because he disobeyed. I dare to differ with them. Here God spoke to Moses and He said,

"Don't hit the rock, but speak to the rock." The Bible clearly shows that Moses was angry with the people. The Bible says that because Moses and Aaron didn't believe, they dishonored God. I did some research on this and the word believe is literally translated, "they did not properly believe." And in not properly believing or showing an example, Moses and Aaron dishonored God. So when the Bible says that Moses didn't believe it literally means because of his anger he showed those people a wrong example of Christian leadership.

Earlier in the book we touched briefly on Moses' other struggles with this spirit. Let's look more in depth at one of those instances: In Exodus 2:11-12, Moses was out walking among the Hebrews. He decided that Pharaoh and the Egyptians were abusing the people of God. He saw an Egyptian hitting an Israelite. The Bible says Moses saw the abuse and he looked this way and that way; saw no one looking at him, so he killed the Egyptian and hid him in the sand. In other words, he knew it was wrong.

We know it's wrong when we hit our spouse. We know it's wrong when we explode. We know it's wrong when we try to manipulate — not with explosive anger but that subtle, manipulating, controlling anger. Like Moses, we may look to see if anybody's watching. We know it's wrong, so we try to bury it in the sand, but God will dig it up and expose it — not to hurt us but to set us free.

God told me, "If your character doesn't change, not only will I not lift you up, I will hold you down." Now we know the scripture, *If God be for us, who can be against us?* (Romans 8:31) But if God be against us, it doesn't matter who be for us. So we can clearly see that dealing with anger is not just a good idea; it is something we absolutely must do because it determines whether or not we will fulfill our divine destiny.

"Good" Anger

In Ephesians 4:26-27, the Word of God says, *"Be angry, and do not sin: do not let the sun go down on your wrath, nor give place to the devil."* This is the Word of God and He says, "be angry, but don't sin." Anger is an emotion that God has given us. Anybody who has never been angry has something wrong with them. Anger is an emotion. Joy is an emotion. Peace is an emotion. God has given us emotions. The word of God says be angry, but don't sin. Be angry but control the anger, don't let the anger control you. Now if God gave us anger, what's anger for? Anger is to be constructive. Uncontrolled anger is destructive.

Let me give you an example. There's an organization called MADD: Mothers Against Drunk Drivers. The organization began when a group of mothers whose children had been killed by drunk drivers said, "You know what? We've lost children, and we're angry enough that we're going to do something so drunk driving will stop." They're changing the way the states look at drunk driving. They are changing the way the nation looks at it. They're changing the way the governments look at it. Their anger is constructive.

Anger is an emotion that gives us a warning. It fuels us to do something to bring about a change. But anger is constructive only when we control it. When it controls us, it can only destroy.

So the Bible says we can be angry and not sin. But when we allow anger to control us — when we move from constructive emotion to destructive emotion — it literally gives permission for the devil to come in and do his job: steal, kill, and destroy. It gives him place.

I'm from an angry background. I'm from an angry family. I'm from an angry neighborhood. Angry people are very aggressive. I have learned to use that anger to become constructive and aggressive toward positive things instead of destructive and aggressive toward negative things.

Anger will kill you. Angry people die early. It is killing you because it is a spirit of destruction. It's not only killing you physically, but it's killing your destiny.

I had an anger problem, but I wasn't so concerned about what it was costing me physically as I was concerned about what it was costing me in my personal life. When I shared this on TBN, Tiz and I got a letter from a man who said he was the victim of anger.

Now when we talk about the victims of abuse, we usually talk about the wife who has been beat up or the children who have been beat up or the person whose boss is abusive and they've lost their job. This guy said, "I'm a victim of abuse also, because I'm the abuser, and I've lost my wife. I've lost my children. I've lost my jobs. I've lost my friends."

Short-term and Long-term Affects of Anger

The reality of it is, there is short-term affect and long-term affect of being a mean and angry person or being a bully. There is a short-term release, but there is a long-term sting. We can bully people by physically controlling them, or we can bully them by emotionally controlling them — also anger. The short-term effect is that everybody is jumping; everybody is cowering; and for the moment, you feel better because you vented yourself. That's the short-term effect.

The long-term effect is that nobody likes you. The long-term effect is that your spouse is going to leave you; your children won't love you; nobody at work wants to work with you; and nobody wants to hire you. When they're getting ready to get rid of somebody at work they're going to get rid of you.

Doctors will tell you it's killing you physically. But folks, the Word of God tells us it's killing us in the long run by stopping every blessing God is trying to bring our way.

The short-term effect is that you feel in control; you feel like you've controlled the situation. In fact, you've controlled everybody but yourself, so you lose. Whether you control physically or emotionally, either way you're out of control. And you lose. We all lose in the long run. God said, "If you don't treat your wife right, I won't hear your prayers. If you don't treat your husband right, I won't hear your prayers." He didn't say, "Husbands, you have to treat your wives right. Don't bully them. But women, you can treat your husbands anyway you want to."

Disciplined Emotion

The Bible does not say that we're not going to feel anger. We are going to feel anger. It's an emotion that God has given us. God's given us a full range of emotions. He doesn't say we should not feel anger, but He does say we need to control our feelings rather than letting them control us.

Feelings — God gave us feelings. He's given us a whole range, but we ought not to have extreme highs and extreme lows. As well as giving us feelings, He's given us an even greater gift. Galatians 5:19-21 says, *"Now the works of the flesh are evident, which are: adultery, fornication, uncleanness, lewdness, idolatry, sorcery, hatred, contentions, jealousies, outbursts of wrath, selfish ambitions, dissensions, heresies, envy, murders, drunkenness, revelries, and the like."* These are works of the flesh. There is no excuse for committing adultery. There's no excuse for worshipping idols. There is no excuse for being jealous, envious, or depressed. No excuse.

Now look at this. Verse 22 says, *"But the fruit of the Spirit is love, joy, peace, longsuffering, kindness, goodness, faithfulness, gentleness, self-control."* See, along with the whole range of emotions that God has given us, He's given us the fruit of the supernatural Spirit, and one aspect of that fruit is self-control.

If our anger is controlling us, then we need to, with the power of God, get back into self-control. Moses didn't have to lose his temper. God told him what to do, and the Bible says God will never ask something of us that we're not able to do with His help. "But," you say, "Moses was irritated." There were times when Jesus was irritated. On one occasion He said, *"How long must I be with you?"* (Mark 9:9) But He didn't punch anybody — physically or emotionally.

God has given us emotions, but He's also given us a spirit of self-control. And that self-control is called discipline. Proverbs 24:30-31 says, *"I went by the field of the lazy man, and by the vineyard of the man devoid of understanding; and there it was, all overgrown with thorns; its surface was covered with nettles; its stone wall was broken down."* Now here's the vineyard that is intended to bring the blessing of God into this man's life. And there it was all torn down. Going on to verse 32, we see the writer's reaction to the vineyard. *"When I saw it, I considered it well; I looked on it and received instruction."* God spoke to me. *"A little sleep, a little slumber, a little folding of the hands to rest; so shall your poverty come like a prowler, and your need like an armed man."* (Proverbs 24:33-34) And when I saw that I said, "Lord, what are you saying to me?" And He said, "Here's this gift this man had. As I went by it, the wall was torn down, the weeds were grown up.

"He's a lazy man. He lacks discipline. It takes discipline to get up and cut your lawn. It takes discipline to sweep your driveway. It takes discipline to wash your clothes. It takes discipline to comb your hair. It takes discipline to shine your shoes. There's nobody who can't do it. It just takes self-control."

That's exactly what God has given us — self-control. It takes discipline not to do what we feel like doing. If we did just what we felt like doing, we would be run by the flesh and not by the Spirit. The Bible tells us to rejoice in the Lord; whether we feel like it or not. He said put on joy, put on happiness.

God won't keep us from doing what we feel like doing, but there's a price to pay. He has given us self-control so we don't have to pay that price. We can feel anger, but we can control anger without it controlling us. We have to do it. God won't do it for you. God won't force you to be happy. God won't make you rejoice. God won't make you believe that all things work together for good.

The short-term affect of anger is that it temporarily makes us feel good. In fact, we call it "blowing off steam." The long-term affect we need to consider carefully is the result of our self-indulgence.

One of the greatest illustrations of the long-term affect of self-indulgence is a man who lost everything because he didn't control what he felt. In Genesis 25 we read this story:

Esau comes in from a hunting trip. As the oldest son of Isaac and the grandson of Abraham, he was the one who carried the birthright of all those greatly blessed generations. But he comes in from hunting and smells a lentil stew Jacob was cooking. And for a temporary appetite, sells his birthright because he felt hungry. He sold all that God had blessed him with for a bowl of beans. I know you're sure you'd never do that, but let me tell you what God showed me. I was selling all that He had blessed me with to fill the appetite of being angry. Now my problem was never depression, my problem was anger. But I was losing my birthright because I wouldn't deal with my anger. God has given us feelings. We can feel these things, but we are to control them. If we let them control us, we will miss out on this final moment of entering into the Promised Land.

God has given you a spirit of self-control. If this is an area where you have often been defeated, don't feel bad or hopeless. It is never hopeless. Feel change. Feel the winds of the Spirit blowing all that away and bringing a miracle from God.

There are some of us who have been angry since we were children. Some of us have felt picked on since we were children. Some of us felt depressed since we were children. But God is telling us in love that we are not children anymore. We're adults. We're men and women of God. There are marriages that you've walked away from because of feelings. There are blessings that you've walked away from. There are things that have been stopped and been pushed away because of feelings. Today God is reminding you that you have the spirit of self-control. The spirit of self-control has been released on you, but you're going to have to receive it and you're going to do something with it.

CHAPTER 10
STOPPING THE STORM OF ANGER

As we saw in a previous chapter, if you're easily offended or if you're an angry person; if your character does not match the fruit of the Spirit, then the Father will put you out of the vineyard because He needs productive vines; ones that bear fruit. If you're an angry person or a bitter person or a sulking person or an unforgiving person, it doesn't mean you won't go to heaven. It just means you won't get to see the blessing of God on this great journey. God will not lift you up above measure.

2 Chronicles 26 clearly illustrates the dangers of self-exaltation and yielding to anger when it is challenged: *"But when he was strong his heart was lifted up, to his destruction, for he transgressed against the LORD his God by entering the temple of the LORD to burn incense on the altar of incense. So Azariah the priest went in after him, and with him were eighty priests of the LORD—valiant men. And they withstood King Uzziah, and said to him, 'It is not for you, Uzziah, to burn incense to the LORD,* [they were warning him about the dangers of stepping outside his measure of faith and his calling] *but for the priests, the sons of Aaron, who are consecrated to burn incense. Get out of the sanctuary, for you have trespassed! You shall have no honor from the LORD God.'* [Now

he was king, which is a good thing. But just because you're king, don't think you can automatically be a priest.] *Then Uzziah became furious; and he had a censer in his hand to burn incense. And while he was angry with the priests, leprosy broke out on his forehead, before the priests in the house of the LORD, beside the incense altar. And Azariah the chief priest and all the priests looked at him, and there, on his forehead, he was leprous; so they thrust him out of that place. Indeed he also hurried to get out, because the LORD had struck him. King Uzziah was a leper until the day of his death."* But what really struck me was the next part of verse 21: *"He dwelt in an isolated house, because he was a leper; for he was cut off from the house of the LORD."*

Now here's a tremendous portion of scripture. Uzziah was a king, anointed and blessed by God, but, just like Moses, he lost everything because of one thing — anger. Now here was a man who was king over all the land, but he lacked self-control. Notice that because of his anger, not only did he get leprosy but also he lived by himself in an isolated house. Angry people will end up being very lonely people. It doesn't matter how much money you have… doesn't matter how much talent you have… doesn't matter how gifted you are. Folks, nobody wants to be around a mean, angry, negative person. Nobody wants to be around them.

I had to deal with this. As I mentioned, I was raised in an angry house. Had an angry attitude. Had an angry spirit. And finally God said, "You know what? It's time to grow up!"

So let's take a look at the strategy He showed me to help overcome this terrible spirit and live in self-control.

Seven Simple Steps to Stopping the Storm of Anger

Number one: You have to admit it.

Before you can go any further, you have to admit that you have an angry spirit. 1 John 1: 9 begins with "If we confess." Now, the problem with an angry person is that he also has a spirit of pride, and pride won't let you admit that you have a problem. Pride is a strange disease. It makes everybody sick except the person who has it. So first of all you have to look at it and admit it. If you're not sure if you're an angry person, ask somebody. Now remember that anger doesn't necessarily mean you go around punching things. That's the obvious form of anger. If you go around punching things or hit your wife or kids, or if you beat up your husband, it is obvious you are a mean and angry person. Those are people who manipulate or control through physical actions.

There are also people who try to control through "micro-management": "Why didn't you call me?" "Where are you?" "Who are you with?" That's control. Or there are those who don't say anything. Have you ever heard (or had) a conversation that sounded something like this: "How are you honey?" "Fine." "Is anything wrong?" "No." "Were you..." "I said nothing!!!" That is also control.

The number one thing is we have to be willing to admit the problem. Now, not confessing or not admitting is as old as the beginning of time. It's not as though you confess to God and He says, "I never knew that! Never knew that about you!" God knows about you. Your husband, your wife, your neighbors know about you. It's not like you're confessing something that nobody knows. If you're an angry, mean person – everybody knows. What God is waiting for is your confession. And if you admit it God takes care of it.

Do you ever think what would have happened if Adam and Eve would have admitted their sin? Picture this: God comes into the Garden and says "Adam where are you?" Now, He knew where Adam was. He knows everything! Then He asked, "What have you done?"

"Nothing."

I wonder if God was trying to heal the whole thing right then, because the next thing He asked was "Have you eaten?" Of course He knows he ate! He watched him. He knows. But what did He say? He said, "Have you eaten?" What if at that point Adam would have answered, "I did it! I ate it! And it wasn't even good!" But what did he do instead? He said, "It was that woman, whom, if I might remind You, YOU gave me". See, the problem with not admitting is that it's always somebody else's fault. "But he makes me so mad; she makes me so mad." Nobody can make you do anything you do not consent to do.

What if Eve would have said, "He's right. I told him that if he wouldn't eat with me, I'd burn his food." What if she would have confessed? But she said, "Wasn't me, it was the snake." See, it's that lying spirit. We think if we lie about it, we're fooling everybody – God included.

I remember when Tiz and I were pastoring in Australia and our son, Luke, was about three years old. We used one of the small bedrooms as my office, and Luke's bedroom was next door. One Saturday night I was working on my sermon. Luke was in bed with all the lights off and was supposed to be asleep. But he had gotten these new little toys, and from his bedroom I could hear the sounds of a pretty incredible small-boy car race, revving engines, speed shifting and all. I said, "Luke." Now I'm telling you, that race came to a halt so fast he actually made the sound of squealing tires. I said, "Luke, go to sleep." There was a pause and this little voice says, "I am asleep." Now you see in that little mind, he thought he could fool me. And in our little minds we think we can fool God, but God knows. He just says "Admit it, confess it, and I will forgive it and wash it away." So step number one is we have to admit it.

Number two: Don't let your anger control you!

Ephesians 4:26 says, *"Be angry, and do not sin: Do not let the sun go down on your wrath."* Be angry and do not sin. You're going to feel anger, but when you feel it, don't yield to it. Take control before it controls you. The verse goes on to say "and don't go to bed mad." You know what happens when you go to bed mad? You mediate on your grievance. It multiples; it grows; it fumes — that molehill will turn into a mountain. So never go to bed angry, because what is a little thing will be blown out of proportion. First it will ruin your sleep, and eventually it will ruin you while the person with whom you are angry doesn't even know what's going on. Your imagination begins to run wild. Then you start tossing and turning, and all that time the other person is sound asleep; totally unaware.

Number three is two rules: First, don't sweat the small stuff and Second, Remember that it's all small stuff!

Think about what it is that makes you mad. Have you ever watched people playing golf or basketball or some other game? Have you seen how mad they get? In the grand scheme of life, how important it is where that ball goes?

When I was a kid in St. Louis, I caddied. The second or third time I caddied was at a luxurious, posh country club with doctors and lawyers. There were four of us caddies and four golfers and we were at a par-three hole. A par three means you go from the tee to the green. On this particular course, the fairway, or the area between the tee and the green, was almost all lake.

The first ball hit by the guy I was caddying went straight into the water. The other three guys are just hollering. They're laughing at him and he's steaming. This guy was either a lawyer or a doctor. Now I mean he surely has more important things on his mind than where that $1 ball went. In the overall view of universe and life: starving children, abused women, and people going to hell, how important is it where that ball goes?

So this guy hits another ball. It goes in the water again. He goes up to edge, drops, and hits another one into the water. He grabs the bag from me and throws his entire bag out into the water. And then I had to go out there and get it. I'm thinking, "Now that's wisdom. He just hit three dollars worth of golf balls into the water, but threw a thousand dollars worth of clubs in there on purpose."

I still have to use self-control when I drive. It drives me nuts how slow people go. I mean... don't they have a life? Don't they have somewhere to go? But, you know, I have to remember number one: don't sweat the small stuff. I know I'm not the only one who gets behind a crawler and just can't wait to pass them. Finally you have opportunity and you get around them and give them one of those swivel-headed glares. So you get way out ahead of them and hit a red light, and here they come, "turtling" up next to you... and all of a sudden you get very busy on your cell phone!

I play golf and I'll hit a ball and it goes anywhere but where I want it to. I'll start to feel that thing rise up. So I say, "You know what, at least we're not in jail. We're not in jail, we're not going to hell — it's a good day." It brings everything right back into alignment. Not in jail, not going to hell — good day.

Number four: Turn your aggression into progression.

Angry people are aggressive people. Turn that aggression from being destructive into being constructive and make progress with your life. You know, it takes a lot of energy to be mad. It takes a lot of energy to fume. Mad people get mad and then they want to share it with everybody. They bring it home with them; serve it as desert at the table.

Take that aggressive nature and all that energy and start setting and reaching goals in your life. One of the reasons people get angry is that they are frustrated. One of the reasons they are frustrated is that their dreams aren't coming to pass. Well, don't have a dream; have a

STOPPING THE STORM OF ANGER

goal. You can have a dream and stay in bed, but to reach a goal you have to get out in the playing field. Take that wasted energy you use being angry or being mad or talking about what happened twenty years ago, and start using it to reach a goal. Turn that destructive energy into constructive energy by setting a goal and get out in the field of life and start accomplishing something.

Number five: The key to not being angry is to love unconditionally.

What does it mean to "love unconditionally?" Jesus said, *"This is My commandment, that you love one another as I have loved you."* (John 15:12) First of all, we're to love all people of all races and all backgrounds. End of story. And you have to decide that. If you're African-American, you cannot let somebody say "Those white people." You must stop them right there. Tell them you won't have that seed put in your spirit. If you're white, you can't let somebody say, "Well, those black people." You can't let somebody come to you and say you need to be with your own kind. You need to turn right around say, "I am with my own kind. I'm with the children of God, born again, washed in the blood." The Bible says we're all looking through a glass darkly, so we need to love each other whether we're white, black, brown, pin-striped, or polka-dotted. If you're white or if your black or you're gypsy or you're Hispanic or you're Asian, don't let somebody tell you that you need to be with your own kind. A kingdom divided against itself cannot stand.

A friend of mine and I were talking about what constitutes a great man of God. He said something that changed my life. He said, "What constitutes a great man or a woman of God is somebody who loves people who can do nothing for them and who can do nothing to them." That's unconditional love. I don't love you because you can help me or hurt me. Jesus said when the rich people come in; don't give them the best seats. Love everybody equally. I believe that's why so many unsaved people come to our church. I believe it is because of one thing: we don't care where people come from, but we're so excited about where they are going. And we want them to enjoy the journey. We love them unconditionally.

Let's say for example, you and your spouse have had several bad years. If you want the blessing of God, you need to forget those things that are behind. If you can't forgive and forget, you haven't forgiven. The Bible says, *"Forgetting those things which are behind."* (Philippians 3:13) So we need to love unconditionally.

Number six: Positive mental attitude.

If you're going to defeat anger, you have to decide 24/7 to have a positive mental attitude. One of Tiz's greatest sayings is, "You're as happy today as you decide to be." If you're only happy when good things are happening, good things won't happen very often, because your attitude always determines your altitude.

You're as happy today as you decide to be. Even if something is happening that doesn't look good, the Bible tells us to rejoice in the Lord always! And then it repeats, "Again I say rejoice!" When you do that, the Lord is at hand. And you can be happy all the time when you decide that all things work together for good.

Now if the Bible is true and we're truly believers, we never have the right to have a bad day. All things work together for good, so we're going to rejoice in the Lord always. and the Bible says that when God sees our faith, He responds. Our faith affects our attitude, and our positive mental attitude, always determines our altitude.

God never said there were no giants. He just said, "I'm a giant killer." But the difficulties aren't there to break you; they're there to make you strong, tempered steel. I love the saying, "With every opportunity there comes difficulties. But with every difficulty there comes opportunities."

David came into the Israeli camp and said, "I have an opportunity to marry the king's daughter." But with that opportunity came the difficulty of killing Goliath. The rest of the camp had a negative mental attitude. They said, "Goliath is too big to defeat." David had a positive mental attitude. He said, "Goliath is too big to miss." It's that simple.

Number seven: Seek the kingdom of God.

When the Bible says, *"Seek first the kingdom of God,"* it means seek God's way. (Matthew 6:33) One of the reasons why people are not happy is because they're frustrated. Frustration turns into anger. The reason we get frustrated is because we are trying to do it our way when God's way is the right way. Is there something that frustrates you? Is there something that makes you angry? The Bible says we are more than conquerors. (Romans 8:37) That means no matter what we're facing, no matter how impossible it seems, if we'll ask God, He will show us the way.

He said, *"My yoke is easy, my burden is light."* (Matthew 11:30) It's when we get out of the will of God that we get frustrated. If you know you're not in the perfect will of God, then at some point you've said no when you should have said yes.

One facet of the will of God is summed up in 3 John 1:2, *"Beloved, I pray that you may prosper in all things and be in health, just as your soul prospers."* Why would we ever want to be outside the will of God? Now when it says we're more than conquerors, it doesn't mean that there won't be some difficulty. Difficulties are not there to break you; they're there to build you.

Jesus endured the cross for the joy that was set before Him. God is asking you to change. God is asking you to deal with anger, deal with being negative. He is asking you to let Him change that spirit for His spirit. Whenever God deals with us about changing, He never promises it will be easy. He just promises it will be worth it.

Changing is not easy, but it is worth it. Facing Goliath was not easy, but out of King David came the birthing of our Lord and Savior. Out of your blessing, out of your anointing, out of God raising you up, in many people's lives will come the birthing of our Lord and Savior. He didn't say it would be easy, but He did say it would be worth it because we are more than conquerors — *more than conquerors* — when we've got Jesus on our side.

For additional copies of this book,
please write to:

Larry Huch Ministries
P.O. Box 610890
Dallas, TX 75261

or visit our website at:

www.larryhuchministries.com

If this book has been a blessing to you,
you may wish to order the CD series
containing more in-depth teaching
on the same subject.

NOTES

NOTES

NOTES

NOTES

NOTES